The Biography of Léon Bloy

Memories of a Friend

I0529413

RENÉ MARTINEAU

Translated By Richard Robinson

Sunny Lou Publishing Company
Portland, Oregon, USA
http://www.sunnyloupublishing.com

1st Edition, Revised & Corrected: July 22, 2022
Original Publication Date: May 13, 2022

ISBN: 978-1-955392-26-6

* * *

This translation from French is based on
the Librairie de France edition of *Léon Bloy (Souvenirs
d'un Ami)*, Paris, 1921.

Contents

Contents

Foreword

In May 2022, three years after the international apocalypse due to the spread of covid-19, – which, to be honest, probably should never have been international at all and should have remained merely a local, if not tragic, affair, at or near its place of origin, which is far from France and the U.S., and where outbreaks of similar viral strains in the last twenty or so years preceding the last one were common enough – I refer to the bird flu outbreak of 1996 and SARS in 2002, – it is very unlikely that we will see the last of these viral problems anytime soon, I regret to say – but I had the good fortune, finally, of being able to return to France again, in order to do some research for another book, but while also finishing up the translation of this one.

All of which might be banal to say if not for the fact that while doing so, and while working with the publisher to produce this book, – I had the opportunity to visit Bourg-la-Reine, outside of Paris, where Léon Bloy had lived the last six or seven years of his life on this planet, which is, if not always, in his own words "adorable," at least still supportable, I think, but maybe less and less so.

I took the RER train from Paris (from the Denfert-Rochereau station, to be exact) and within twenty minutes *approximativement*, as the train slowed down to stop, I was able to catch a glimpse of, from behind the windows of the station at Bourg-la-Reine, the back of the head of the patinated bronze statue of André Theuriet, former mayor of the town, still sitting in his chair and holding a rose. It was a warm feeling of satisfaction and I felt like other friends of Léon Bloy must have felt, who had come to visit him, over one hundred years earlier, and according to his indications:

> *You will pass before a mediocre statue*
> *of a ridiculous man, then you will see*
> *the trees and the blue chairs and final-*
> *ly you will see me, me, with my friend*
> *Martineau, and perhaps also my god-*
> *son Pierre...*

Martineau and Pierre were no longer there, at least not in person, when I arrived, and neither were the garish-blue chairs which, if I was not mistaken, should have stood somewhere behind the tall, garish-green metal fences erected (how long ago?) across the street and in front of the statue.

From there I walked towards what I guessed to be the center of town, in the direction of place Condorcet – *3, place Condorcet, Bourg-la-Reine,* to be precise, where Bloy had resided.

> *M. and Mme. Léon Bloy have the hon-*
> *or of informing you that from May 15,*
> *1911 they will be domiciled at 3, place*
> *Condorcet, Bourg-la-Reine.*

Along the way, I met on the sidewalk a delightful elderly lady, Lucia Mariani-Chehab, who was on her way to do some grocery shopping. She is an author herself of prose, poetry and translations, including

Les lettres à Jeanette. She gave me directions. We spoke for about five minutes standing and chatting, and eventually lamenting the lack of readers in the world, our own and in general, and although she had never heard of Léon Bloy herself, I do not and did not hold it against her – for no one in that town seems to have heard of him, save the several individuals who work at the cemetery.

I found 3, place Condorcet easily enough then, with Lucia's assistance, and I was delighted to see a plaque on the wall of the building, commemorating the great writer's having lived there, on the 2nd floor (3rd floor in English).

After spending a few minutes "reflecting" in front of his old habitation, in front of which stretched a small square of grass and trees, several wooden benches, and even a covered merry-go-round, I set out on foot to visit the cemetery. Along the way, I passed a bookstore and decided to enter it to see what books, if any, they carried by the master. They carried not a one. I asked the woman behind the counter for more information, and had to spell the author's name for her when she said "Qui?" (Who?). No, no, assuredly not, they did not carry any of Léon Bloy's works. "Poor Léon Bloy," I thought to myself before exiting. The conspiration of silence continues today, even in the small town where once he lived, a few blocks away from his last residence, – residences...

At the cemetery, I found his grave or humble "tomb" and purchased, from across the street, a pot of geraniums to place on his last resting place. For there were merely pebbles there where his body once lay, and also an old (though not dead) succulent, which was surprisingly appropriate given those plants' resiliency to long periods of drought. The bright pink or red geraniums brightened things up and made his memorial more cheerful.

And that's all I have to say on the matter, fair reader of half of dozen. René, Léon, and myself are grateful to have you. Oh, one more thing:

In the introduction to this book, René Martineau says

> *Salvation Through The Jews* (1892), *The Woman Who Was Poor* (1897), *Sueur de Sang* (1893), and the *The Ungrateful Beggar* (1898) are the books I would suggest overall to whomever wants to come into contact with Léon Bloy.

I would add to that list, or replace it with, these: *The Desperate Man*, *Salvation Through The Jews, Blood of the Poor, She Who Weeps*, and *The Soul of Napoleon,* in that order.

Que Léon Bloy soit béni!

– Richard Robinson, 2022 May 14.

Dedication

For my dear Anne-Marie, who admired Léon Bloy as I admired him and who knows, better then I do, the essential of that great soul. – R.M.

Note to the Reader

I will not pretend to explain Léon Bloy in this work. Not having known the author of *The Desperate Man* except during the last eighteen years of his life, I have also not attempted to write his complete biography.

I have wanted only to relate what I have seen, to repeat what I have heard him say about himself, to show the simplicity and the generosity of that great visionary and great artist who has so often been accused of being complicated and lacking in charity, also to provide some information regarding the books that I have seen him publish; all that, of course, in addition to his journal which I have no desire to rectify, but which I can annotate, having much frequented the author, having greatly loved him, and possessing an unbounded admiration for him.

The last three chapters of the present book are the veritable result of my enterprise. I preceded them by "Léon Bloy's Beginnings," the article that appeared while Bloy was still alive, its having been read and absolutely approved by him, and which includes several pages on his first days spent in Denmark, in 1891.

He had spoken to me about that trip in a very particular manner, and as he had mentioned it nowhere else that I know of, I thought it of interest to mention it here.

All this could not be published without the accompaniment of a summary of Léon Bloy's childhood and the years that preceded our encounter. That comprises the material of the Introduction.

Finally, I must address my respectful thanks to Madame Bloy for all that she has added to my observations, while drawing from her personal memories, and I humbly request of all those who have responded to my questions regarding Léon Bloy to believe in my total recognition of their cooperation.

Introduction

Léon Bloy was born in Périgueux, July 11, 1846. What his childhood was like, he alone could have informed us, but it was a subject that he did not willingly entertain his friends with. He was still a small child when his parents were surprised by his violence and by his tears. For he would often cry in terror at the mere idea that he had schoolmates and masters, in ravishment at the sight of an April sun and the apple trees in bloom and also for no known reason, but simply because he was gifted with a profundity and with melancholy. His father was a freethinker. The child, although not very sentimental by nature, found in the presence of his very Christian mother a comfort for his sadness, and religious practices held an attraction for him.

That future champion of Catholicism was a Catholic from childhood, and if, a little while after his twentieth birthday, the admiration that he had for Barbey d'Aurevilly made him fall in love even more with piety and proselytism, there was nothing of a conversion involved, but the simple development of principles that had always been with him.

"I haven't had much success around Catholics," he used to say, "for not having been a convert!"

In high school in Périgueux, inconceivable fights abounded. Léon Bloy returned home each day covered in blood, when he wasn't brought home three-quarters dead.

His father, a rigid man and very taken with the theories of his day concerning education, had to withdraw him from his fourth year at highschool, asking himself with growing anxiety what would become of a son for whom every social contact seemed impossible and who, besides, made no progress, incapable as he was of submitting to regular tasks.

At eighteen, Léon Bloy declared that he wanted to become a painter and manifested astonishing gifts that should have been revelatory of his genius, but inspired nothing but suspicion and desolation.

The paternal household, called Le Fenétreau, was situated in a faubourg of Périgueux, the faubourg Saint-Georges, where a small river, the Isle, winds through it; Bloy's first drawings are a reproduction of the old willow trees bordering the river; the greater part of those drawings are remarkable and contain, very apparently, qualities that will be those of the writer. After a number of hesitations, the young man was allowed to enter into apprenticeship with an architect who was collaborating then on the construction of the gare d'Austerlitz [in Paris]. It was a way of reconciling a practical education and Léon Bloy's artistic predilections. He was even allowed to attend the atelier de Pils where scenes from Périgueux high school nearly started all over again, tragically, Bloy having decided to defend himself from the *bullies* with a knife.

By the end of a year, he had left the architect's office and the painter's workshop. He then entered into apprenticeship with a solicitor.

He grew bored, did not allow himself to be seduced by any of the Parisian distractions, profited by a reduction accorded by the Compagnie d'Orléans to its employees in order to travel to Périgueux every Sunday to embrace his parents, while undergoing two nights of travel by train, there and back.

His ideas were often in contradiction with those of his father. That meticulous man did not go easy with his advice. He wrote to him, on June 20, 1864, the following letter. One may easily guess at his father's detailed and demanding spirit, which Bloy, an absolute and categorical artist, could hardly subscribe to:

> *My dear Léon,*
>
> *I do not wish to delay responding to your letter.*
>
> *We were waiting for news from you with an impatience that you cannot imagine. M. P*** told me that he has seen you two times, but that hardly gave us much to go on.*
>
> *I am quite happy to hear of your being on good terms with M. Leroux. They will become better still when you do your best. Don't forget then any of his recommendations, write to me about them, pay attention to what goes on around you and turn it to your advantage; be complaisant, being considerate to all those you work with.*

If they are gay and mock you, laugh louder than they do, but do not respond except by courteous means. If there is someone you do not like, examine your conscience to make sure you are not at fault, even if involuntarily. Limit yourself to being reserved with him, in your affability, but always be polite. You will have everyone on your side and more often than not even that little annoyance will go away on its own. You are keeping your journal, doubtless. Keep me abreast of your progress of every sort and tell me even the praises and reprimands that you receive. My perfect knowledge of every detail will facilitate the observations that I can make to you and the advice that I can give you as to what you need to do to perfect yourself.

I have no time right now to write to Mme. L***, whom I desire that you should meet, but at the first free moment I have, I will write to that good and excellent lady whom you remember, I think.

There is nothing new in my situation. I have just seen M. Krantz who finds fault with you for not having approached him. Your mother is here and always suffering. I have not yet received any news from Paul. I think that you have written to him. Georges continues to believe that he will be accepted at the school in Angers. Your aunt, Marc, Henri, Jules are just as you left them.

Tell me how you spend your time at school, what you do, with details. Tell me what you do at the office, the difficulties that you have encountered, etc.

Soon you will need to think about furniture. Plan in advance and take possession of your lodgings as soon as possible. Buy what is necessary to start and, once you have moved in, follow up with what is necessary, then with what is comfortable, which is also necessary so that you can love the nest that you have chosen.

Goodbye, my dear child, I need to stop now for your mother has asked me to leave her half a page. Say hello to M. Renaud for me and if, as I imagine, you pay a visit soon to Mme. Renaud, pay her my respects.

One more thing, when you pay her a visit, think a bit on what you need to say, say it simply and don't overstay your visit; in Paris, life is busy and those who stay long become a nuisance.

Your friend and father, ...

– *BLOY*.

In Paris, Léon Bloy hooked up with Georges Landry with whom he shared a room, on rue Rousselet. A book publisher, whom Léon Bloy had some business with, pointed out Barbey d'Aurevilly to him, whom he did not know and whom also, consequently, he did not know that he was neighbors with.

It was then that Léon Bloy wrote an article that he resolved to submit to the master.

The latter received the debutant with his habitual good-naturedness, and that was the beginning of a friendship that ended only with Barbey's death.

In 1870, Léon Bloy joined the irregular corps de Cathelineau.

What follows is a letter that his mother wrote to him at that time, as different a letter as could be imagined from that of his father cited earlier. It will give a complete idea of Léon Bloy's origins and youth:

24 October 1870.

My dear Léon,

I am hurrying up to write to you, I would like you to receive several lines from me, for I have need to tell you all the wishes of my poor heart and all the supplications that it will address to Heaven so that you might return to me. Ah! dear child, I want also to bless you and to protect you the mo-

ment you find yourself exposed to danger; a poor mother's benediction is always followed by that of God; receive it then, this benediction. May God never stop protecting you, may the Holy Virgin, our good Mother, and all the holy angels accompany you and watch over you. My heart follows my benediction, it seems to me as though it goes with it, my poor child, I embrace you, would that it be not the last time!

May God's will be done and not mine!

You will be, I have no doubt about it, worthy of the choice that has fallen on you to bring forward. I am also as happy as you are that you have joined the corps de Cathelineau.

Goodbye, my dear son, if we should never see each other again on earth, we will be together again soon in Heaven.

Your mother,

— MME. BLOY.

    P.S. (in the father's handwriting): Whatever happens, do your duty and be blessed.

— BLOY

With his memories of the war, Léon Bloy wrote one of his masterpieces: *Sueur de Sang.*

He endured, moreover, the fatigues of the campaign better than others. When he spoke to me, much later, about the prodigious strength that was attributed to him, he told me, "It's a legend, if not a joke; but I was an indefatigable marcher. During the retreat to Mans, I carried a comrade who could no longer stand up on his own. And I had, in addition to that advantage, another which was to be in possession of an exceptional stomach. I remained for an entire day without eating, and the following day I could wolf down a sumptuous meal without any problem."

After the war, Bloy returns to inhabit rue Rousselet and resumes, for his old master, the proof-reader job that he shared with M. Landry. In 1874, he published two articles in *l'Univers*, and immediately thereafter Barbey d'Aurevilly, having a premonition of the artist, encourages Léon Bloy, spurs him on.

Bloy is completely surprised. Habituated from a very early age to doubt himself, he could not come to a decision, despite his trust in Barbey's judgment, to undertake a work of any length.

In 1877, he wrote *La Chevalière de la Mort*, several pages which he admits to be imitations of Carlyle and which he did not dare publish until 1891 in a small review in Ghent.

He was familiar then with all the writers who frequented Barbey d'Aurevilly and very particularly Féval and Hello who love him and see talent in the least of his essays.

But they know nothing about his real life, the exclusively contemplative existence he led from 1878 to 1882. To get an idea of it, one must read *The Desperate Man* and fill in the autobiography with some guess work.

If Léon Bloy's friends, in 1878, knew nothing about that history, his friends of today are no more the wiser. Léon Bloy did not like it when people brought it up, and it's a subject that I constantly avoided bringing up with him.

In 1882, he begins resolutely to focus on his work. His confidence, however, is not absolute, for he proceeds merely in the wake of the Count Roselly de Lorgues by publishing *The Revealer of the Globe*, a work of exegesis which Barbey d'Aurevilly wrote the preface to.

That same year, Bloy becomes, at the *Chat Noir*, a collaborator of Salis and Emile Goudeau and, in a matter of weeks, he is famous, at least within the Parisian literary world.

That was then, for him, the beginning of the torments and tribulations that engendered the particular bitterness that made him unacceptable to his colleagues.

What was the exact essence of that grief, of that torment which, until his last years, tortured him?

I have in front of my eyes a copy of *The Desperate Man* furnished with this dedication:

> *The worst human torment is the thirst*
> *for Grandeur and Beauty, and there*
> *are poor poets who suffer for thirst as*

much as guilty Angels can suffer...

> *Ah! It is not the world's contempt that tortures them, it is exile from the paternal House and the necessity those miserable wretches have to watch over the loathsome swine whose nourishment they are reduced to envying.*

> *The author of* The Desperate Man *was familiar with that excessive misfortune, and he will be familiar with it doubtless unto his dying day. It is for that reason that he begs pity from hearts on the highways and in the corner of the woods, being, besides, always armed to the teeth[1].*

One could attribute that thought to Baudelaire, with the exception of the last words which modify it in a very telling manner.

The grief attributed to rubbing shoulders with ugliness and impossible mediocrities that must be fled from is at the foundation of Léon Bloy's sufferings. It's the same grief common to all poets.

But his naïvety having made him suppose for one instant that intellectual milieus could provide, if not for his soul, at least for his mind, a sort of refuge or abandon, he entered upon them boldly only to run away from them soon thereafter, not without having left behind the appearance of a contempt that many

[1]The worst... armed to the teeth: from a Dedication of a reprint of the *The Desperate Man* to Elisabeth Joly. See the August 17, 1913 entry in *The Threshold to the Apocalypse: 1913-1915*.

have not forgiven him for.

Since then, he has enemies, which explains the last phrase of that dedication cited just now, wherein he believes it necessary to arm himself both offensively and defensively. Lambast becomes for Léon Bloy the only form in which journalism can be conceived.

He demonstrates qualities in his journalism that were unknown prior to him, a verve of incomparable power, a manner of belittling his adversary who appears incapable of a reply, situated from then on in a ridiculous and dangerous posture. The entirety of those articles, almost all of which appeared in the *Chat Noir*, forms two volumes: *Words of a Demolitions Contractor*, and *Belluaires et Porchers*, to which must also be added a small review, *Le Pal*, which had but four issues only (1885).

The first of the two volumes was published in 1884, immediately after *The Revealer of the Globe*, and the second one much later, in 1905.

The author was, at the time of his first books, admired by several men of letters only, but admired passionately. He told himself that his lambasts had partially succeeded and that by a doubling-down of force and energy he could attain perhaps a wider success. He introduced lambast into the novel form with *The Desperate Man*.

That book, in ten years from now, will not appear anywhere as terrible as it appears to us today, nor moreover as it appeared to its first readers: "It is nothing more," Léon Bloy told me, "than a bundle of brushwood on fire."

Whatever the case might be, *The Desperate Man* is still the most famous book by the author, who showed himself for the first time by his particular qualities of a Catholic writer.

It is with that autobiography that he begins, according to his expression, *to play on his soul as on a supernatural violin and one has never heard so sorrowful a music before.*

To the suffering of the poet will be added another suffering. Léon Bloy no longer sees anything but souls: his soul and the souls of other men. His anger becomes, in his own words, the effervescence of his pity, and it will manifest through his books which he knows, by these acts, to be his mission.

From an unpublished letter, written six years ago, I copy this:

> *You will have no doubt heard about the Communion of Saints, but without anyone having explained to you that because you now belong to Jesus Christ as an essential member of his divine Body, being from now on not only a participant but identified, that is to say, God himself in that manner and God the redeemer, there are human creatures of unknown numbers who depend on you, needing to be assisted and saved by you.*

> *The Communion of Saints, antidote or counterpart to the Dispersion of Babel, attests to so divine and so marvelous a human solidarity that it is impossible for a human being not to be answerable for all the others, in the time they live, have lived, or will have to live...*

To those who pass through life satisfied, and their conscience empty, he cries:

> *Poor wretch, don't you realize that you have an immortal soul and that that very soul contains an abyss of mystery!*
>
> *Each man has his gulf which he does not know, which he cannot know...*[2]

The desire to reach souls with his books became for Léon Bloy almost the one and only goal of his vocation. In *The Woman Who Was Poor*, which appeared in 1897, he demonstrated his genius as an artist and went so far as to write:

> *... I am not an artist... I am a pilgrim of the Holy Sepulcher. Unimaginable skies have no other use to me than to mark the place of an old stone where Jesus slept for three days.*
>
> *Born for my indescribable desolation in a phantom century where that rudimentary notion has been totally for-*

---

[2] Original footnote: from an unpublished letter.

> *gotten, could I do any better than pick*
> *up the stick of old travelers who be-*
> *lieved in the accomplishment of the*
> *Word of God?*[3]

The people of the century did not hear the vociferator who redoubled with violence.

Wishing to break all the idols, he attacked all reputations. They avenged themselves on him by continuing to starve him: he became poor.

From that moment forward, the comparison with other poets, with Baudelaire for example, is no longer possible.

Léon Bloy is a dandy in reverse who takes great pride in his rags. He was familiar with the voluptuousness of the suffering that he had accepted for the love of God: "All that happens in life is adorable," he wrote, "and I am seared by the tears!"

He is of course declared impossible, incomprehensible, and what's more, by his attitude, he insults not only the indifferent or the triumphant, but also their one and veritable god, riches.

He is detested.

Poverty became a misery for Léon Bloy, a frightful misery that forced him to beg.

His *Journal*, which comprises seven volumes, is made from the history of his infinite tribulations. In his day-to-day notes, the author loses nothing of his qualities. Curious thing that those will be the pages by

---

[3]Original footnote: *The Woman Who Was Poor*, p. 225.

which the larger public will get to know him, those pages that procured for him the several thousands of readers that he has had for over ten years now.

For it must be said, if his misery was real, his dereliction was not absolute. To the cries that he let out before the crowd, several beings stopped and listened to him.

In 1890, he had married the daughter of Danish poet Christian Molbech and not only did that admirable Christian know how to share and attenuate his sufferings, but she also understood Léon Bloy's work and gave to him the exclusive admiration, exempt of restrictions, that he was thirsting for.

To the faithful few who came and joined his wife and daughters, to place their soul in the shadow of his soul, Léon Bloy spoke more particularly of the mystery:

> *Penetrated, haunted, possessed by the certitude that all is mysterious, men and things, because symbolist or figurative, I wanted to demonstrate everywhere the mystery that is always evident for me and to make it felt with an extreme violence, to the point of producing a constriction and dilation of hearts...*[4]

Salvation Through the Jews and, later, *Blood of the Poor*, *The Soul of Napoleon*, *Joan of Arc and Germany*, *Meditations of a Solitary in 1916*, and *In The*

---

[4] Original footnote: unpublished letter.

Tenebrae, this latter, alas, left unfinished, are the result of that enormous effort of exegesis.

Certain people have reproached him clumsily for speaking of those things while being ignorant of theology, forgetting that Léon Bloy had never pretended to position himself as a theologian. He knew above all what cannot be taught, what is missing so completely by so many theologians:

> *I know, he said, that I am a clairvoyant in the thickest darkness and a blindman in the dazzlement of the light...*

Let's admire, at the very least, the extraordinary language that he knew how to create in order to treat of those extraordinary subjects that became more and more familiar to him, in proportion as the causes of distress accumulated on his head.

The visible world appeared hideous and benighted to him, the invisible world full of beauty and brightness.

Mme. J. Termier-Boussac has magnificently captured that arresting face of the genius of Léon Bloy, and I cannot help citing this example of the sensibility of a poet penetrated by another poet:

> *One had ideas, notions that one believed to be clear; one had evaluated for oneself, for better or for worse, a metaphysic, harmonizing the universe in one's fashion, putting each thing in its place and deliberately putting to*

> *bed the Unknowable so as no longer*
> *to be disquieted. The least dogmatic*
> *and most profound among us are like*
> *that and carry away in their mind*
> *analogous puerile constructions.*
>
> *Léon Bloy destroys that organization*
> *and those presumed clarities. It's one*
> *of the most remarkable characteristics*
> *of his genius, that power to enrich*
> *mystery, to immediately stretch the*
> *bounds of the subjects he treats of. He*
> *raises before our eyes his own apper-*
> *ception of the world, no longer precise*
> *and linear, but chaotic and shattered,*
> *fissured by new gulfs unimagined until*
> *then.*

To consider Léon Bloy's work in that way, we find
ourselves far, very far indeed from the lambasting
pamphleteer, a denomination that ended by annoying
him:

> *Ah! I'm not that person; however, he*
> said, *and when I was like that, it was*
> *for indignation and love and my cries,*
> *– I let them out in despair over my*
> *shattered ideal ...*

One must not think, in fact, that Léon Bloy felt only
at ease vociferating violences. Nobody, on the contrary, possessed a greater variety of tones of voice. He
knew how to be sweet and gentle, and how to make
his gentleness persuasive, caressing, and enveloping,
as necessary.

An artist, he was not an irreducible force going in every direction, in the search of whatever it might be; he knew how to temper his expression, to set his quill in diapason with that supernatural instrument that was his soul.

He lost his composure only in the face of a poorly expressed work and, for that reason, he has not always been an exact critic.

One knows the phrase by Ernest Hello: "Present to a mediocre man his own ideas expressed with splendor, and he will not recognize them!..."

Léon Bloy endured, for the opposite reason, an analogous impression. A man of genius, you can present to him his own ideas deprived of splendor, but he will not recognize them anymore, and never did his judgment become more acerbic than before a ridiculous or obscure expression.

The thing is that he attached to form the importance that it merited.

He knew that one does not persuade by reasonings alone, but by beauty. His writing, which resembled a vigorous and perfected drawing, illustrating that he had been an illuminator, is indicative of that constant desire that tormented him of being luminous in his least productions.

The culminating point of his genius is at the center of his work: *Salvation Through The Jews* (1892), *The Woman Who Was Poor* (1897), *Sueur de Sang* (1893), and the *The Ungrateful Beggar* (1898) are the books I would suggest overall to whomever wants to come into contact with Léon Bloy.

The Exegesis of Commonplaces, begun in 1899 and published in 1902 is a misunderstood masterpiece.

That the author had seen the need to add to those marvelously successful pages several stories that one might find a bit too heavy, was a lapse of good judgment – I will be the first to admit it. But the volume, and I am referring to the first in the series,[5] is nonetheless a model of vanquished difficulty.

Baudelaire had glimpsed the literary means to express his disgust for the epoch he lived in.

Flaubert indicated even a vague plan for a book such that as soon as one had read it one would no longer dare to speak, for fear of repeating, without thinking about it, a phrase found in it.[6]

Both had divined the originality of such a work without illusions as to the difficulty there would be in executing it.

Léon Bloy had deployed in that space a verve worthy of those greatest ironists joined to a surety in the psychology that they have rarely attained.

As for all works whose originality is of the first order, one must go back very far into the history of literature to find a possible comparison. By proceeding thus, Léon Bloy's book has always made me

---

[5]Original footnote: A second series came out in 1913.

[6]Original footnote: Edouard Maynial: *Flaubert's Youth*. Mercure de France.

think of the comedies by Aristophanes who repeats the word *demos* as frequently as the author of *The Exegesis of Commonplaces* wrote the word *bourgeois*.

Of course, in *Exegesis*, there is something else, for it is a Christian work and in reality, by Léon Bloy's own admission, the most dolorous work he ever produced.

I have called *Sueur de Sang* among the four best works written by the author. The collection of thirty stories, all which appeared in the *Gils Blas* and were written with the memories of that war of '70 which Bloy participated in, as I have already said, constitutes a veritable prophesy. Bloy saw the Germans such as they were and such as they are, abject and appalling. Why is this volume, reprinted recently, not in every French person's hands?

I will speak later about books written since we met in 1901.

In that period, the best of that enormous, variable, and picturesque work had already appeared, work full of cries of revolt or enthusiasm, made with ingenuity and profundity, inspired by suffering and nevertheless sane, containing an inalterable and sublime optimism.

He has been called unclassifiable. From the single point of view of literature, it is not however impossible to categorize him.

Léon Bloy, in fact, belongs to the generation of artists that immediately followed the Romantic period, and he is himself a Romantic as are all the writers of that same epoch who possess a certain value. He is a Romantic just like Barbey d'Aurevilly, Baudelaire, and Villiers.

He was, like them, constantly in search of images, and, as Remy de Gourmont remarked a long time ago,[7] nobody found them in so great an abundance as he did.

When poetry becomes completely internal and lyricism is extinguished, one admitted only what one might call, as he did in *The Son of Louis XVI*: "The blues eyes of French monarchy."

On the other hand, J.-K. Huysmans, in search of *Californian*[8] epithets, trembled with joy before that phrase written by Bloy, with respect to *A rebours*:

> *"… His mode of expression, always armed and exhibiting defiance, never suffers restraint, not even that of its mother Image, which it outrages with the vaguest desire of tyranny and which it drags behind itself continually, by the hair or by the feet, down the worm-eaten stairway of frightened Syntax."*

It is said that Huysmans, several hours after having read that phrase for the first time, went along repeating it: "… the worm-eaten stairway of frightened Syntax."

---

[7]Original footnote: *Le Livre des Masques:* Léon Bloy.

[8]Californian: in the El Dorado sense of word with also a hint of the heat and furnace contained in the name.

In Léon Bloy's first books, written at the beginning his career, the several instances of poor taste that one encounters, and which he himself admitted to however, are the faults of Romanticism: there is at the beginning of *The Desperate Man* the entire story of a lost child and also the episode with Véronique having her teeth pulled out, – pure melodrama. Finally, certain stories in *Histoires désobligeantes* are equally loaded with inventions that the beauty of the language renders all the more apparent.

The author recognized quickly the need to completely avoid those Romantic abuses. They are no longer found in *The Woman Who Was Poor*, which Léon Bloy judges, rightly, as being superior to the two books previously mentioned.

He loved lyricism provided that the subject of the poem was not at all sentimental. Of all the poets that he had read, I never heard him cite others besides Baudelaire and Hugo.

He had a huge contempt for Alfred de Musset.

One day when I was telling him to try not thinking about it, before he left on a trip that seemed to him extremely painful, he began to recite, very softly:

> *Vois sur ces canaux*
> *Dormir ces vaisseaux*
> *Dont l'humeur est vagabonde.*
> *C'est pour assouvir*
> *Mon moindre désir.*[9]

---

[9]*Vois... désir.* From "Invitation to the Voyage," by Charles Baudelaire. "Look at those canals/where those vessels

And he added: "That's very beautiful..."

It's generally not known that he had read almost all of Léon Gozlan. He had even re-read him as a kind of recreation. The very titles of books written by that novelist were enough to make him joyful. To serious people who spoke to him of even more serious subjects, he said: "Am I right in thinking that you are not familiar with *Le Vampire du Val-de-Grâce?*..."

But his favorite books, those for which he had unfailing admiration, were *The Bewitched, The Future Eve, Tribulat Bonhomet* and stories like *l'Intersigne* and *Akédysséril*[10] whose perfection enchanted him.

That short enumeration will suffice to illustrate Léon Bloy's Romantic tastes. That was not the only genre he often read. He often read from *The Bible* and always in Latin. And also Juvenal; and the works of the blessed Catherine Emerick, Catherine Emerick's life story, *Travels in Tartary* by M. Huc, etc.

Le latin mystique, by Remy de Gourmont, pleased him to no end, and he wrote an enthusiastic article on that book.

Of everything that was written about him, Léon Bloy, he liked best the several very fine and

---

slumber/whose spirits are restless./It's to assuage/my least desire[/that they come here from the ends of the earth].

[10]*The Bewitched... Akédysséril*: the first is a novel by Barbey d'Aurevilly; the rest are works by Villiers de l'Isle-Adam.

very eloquent pages that Mme. Rachilde had consecrated[11] to the first volume of his *Journal*. "Nothing,"
he often said to me, "was more helpful." It is perhaps,
in fact, thanks to that noble homage by Rachilde that
the public fell in love, in a certain way, with Léon
Bloy's *Journal*.

Since his death, his name has been placed beside that of Villiers de l'Isle-Adam and Barbey d'Aurevilly, assigning him a nearly equivalent place beside
those two great geniuses.

But, for Léon Bloy to have his true place, we
will need to wait a little while longer. We will need to
wait for the eternal side of his work to have gained
the upper hand on the story of the realities of a day.

The men of our time are too much the slaves
of their opinions and their prejudices not to confound
with intransigence what was merely the excess of individualism.

Modern Catholics will never admit, with very
few exceptions maybe, that a love for God could have
dictated the remonstrances that Léon Bloy made to
his curate, and there is no freethinker who will line up
behind an artist who received daily communion.

The one and the other do not like naïvety, holy
anger, prophesies, ecstasies and, in general, anything
outside practical life.

What remains is the lambasting pamphleteer
whom one understands better, but whom one understands only by attaching an entire range of unpardon-

---

[11]Original footnote: *Mercure de France*, June 1898.

able defects to his character.

Having known Léon Bloy for only the last twenty years of his life more or less, I cannot say whether, anteriorly, he had made himself as unsupportable as some have said.

As for myself, I can state, without fear of gainsay by the friends that he had, that there was never a more affectionate or tender man.

In the most difficult moments that he passed through, it really did not take a lot to console him and to appease him.

In his moments of tranquility, he was rather happy and his conversation was as full of jokes as it was of deep thoughts.

He was a very generous man, that beggar, and capable, as it happened, of depriving himself of enormous sums of money, relative to what he possessed at the moment when he gave them.

Free of prejudice, indulgent even, he received people very simply, careful not to aggrieve his interlocutor in any way. For Léon Bloy to burst out vehemently, some importunate individual was needed.

Unknown for a long time, he has been spoken of in terms of high praise for several years now. His work has been reprinted, people collect his books, he has been sought after in original editions. His enemies have bowed down before the power of his genius, growing disquieted by what he published. Success, although it was never very profitable for him materially, diminished the bitterness of his last years.

Until then, he had to support the *ennui*, the worries, the insults, even the bitterness with nothing but patience and courage which in no way indicated a severe or sullen character. He said of himself, and correctly, that the particular characteristic of his nature was tenderness and contemplation. I am tempted to add: and good humor!

Léon Bloy's Early Years

The beauty of Léon Bloy's work consists in this: that it had to be accomplished in suffering and abandonment.

On that score, it has often been said that there existed in the world only a handful of people insightful enough to have understood him and bold enough to call out what they saw.

It seems to me however that not enough attention has been placed on something more astonishing still – that his constancy in battle and his acceptation of suffering, it is Peace, a profound Peace in the midst of which all the prodigies of that existence are fulfilled.

When Léon Bloy met a suffering or abandoned soul, he said to him: "Follow me, with me you have nothing to fear."

That Peace, which is found on all the pages of his journal, which one feels to be ever present, which creates in the vicinity of the worst distresses an inalterable good humor and, in parallel with the most violent lambasts, a manner, so very French, of translating the tenderest and most affectionate of feelings, – that Peace was not given to Léon Bloy, a man of goodwill, except after years of tribulations and effort.

Also, after having read the last volume of Léon Bloy's journal, while considering what is called, in our own days, a literary life, – the astonishing prostitution of talent, the unbelievable cuisine of contemporary journalism, criticism and the novel, – one asks oneself with curiosity what the early years of this genial artist must have been like; one would like to have even another volume, a prologue to *The Ungrateful Beggar* wherein his first attempts were recounted.[12]

Here is, however, in the absence of such a volume, an interesting chapter in the life of Léon Bloy. One will see in it that his genius as a writer was prefigured in an epoch when he had hardly bothered with publishing books.

> *I entered upon literary life at thirty-eight years of age – he wrote[13] – after an appalling youth and following an indescribable catastrophe that compelled me to escape an exclusively contemplative existence. I entered upon it like the disgraced elect might enter into a hell of filth and obscurity, flagellated by a Cherub by implacable necessity.* Angelus Domini coarctans me.[14] *On seeing my hideous new companions, the horror transuded me*

---

[12]volume, a prologue: *The Desperate Man,* in fact, as well as some of the articles in *The Words of a Demolitions Contractor,* could be seen in part as that earlier journal.

[13]Original footnote: *My Journal,* p. 61 – Letter to O. Mirbeau.

[14]*Angelus... me*: Latin for "The Angel of God constraining me." A slight version of a line from Psalm 34: "Angelus Domini coarctans eos."

> *through every pore. How is it possible*
> *that my literary attempts would have*
> *turned out any other way, filled with*
> *sobs and hurlings?*

The exclusively contemplative existence that Léon Bloy speaks of lasted precisely from the years 1878 to 1882, and those people who knew Léon Bloy well, know that his true basis is tenderness and contemplation. So, in 1879, he paid very little attention to being this or that outside of his contemplative life and did not hope or desire to be understood.

Paul Féval, Ernest Hello, his friends at that time, were completely in the dark as to that luminous existence of his.

Barbey d'Aurevilly himself did not divine it.

As early as 1874, the author of *The Bewitched* had a premonition of the artist:

"If you don't put yourself to the task, I will have a falling out with you," he wrote to him... and he had a hundred good reasons to want to encourage Léon Bloy, who had an unbounded confidence in Barbey d'Aurevilly's judgment and no confidence in himself.

La Chevalière de la Mort, written in 1877,[15] was not even considered by its author as a conclusive experience; it was only much later, in 1884, at the

---

[15]Original footnote: It was published in 1891 by a publisher in Ghent. – A run of 100 very rare copies, reprinted by the *Mercure de France* in 1896.

Chat Noir journal, that Léon Bloy began to think of himself as a writer.[16]

In 1879, he was inhabiting, on rue Rousselet, in the neighborhood of Barbey d'Aurevilly, a small paved room, completely empty, where he did not even have a bed.

Léon Bloy stretched out, over the bricks, an old worm-eaten counterpane of indescribable thinness. He lived without heat, even during the frightful winter of 1879-80. In that period of misery, he invariably wore winter clothing in the summer and summer clothing in the winter.

Paul Féval sometimes came, all the way from Montmartre to rue Rousselet, to bring him assistance; he cherished Léon Bloy.

They had met for the first time at the beginning of that year, 1879, on the occasion of an article that Léon Bloy had come to read to Féval, the which had been very surprised by the article and very impressed by the visitor.

That article was a vehement response by Léon Bloy to an injurious criticism by Pontmartin on the occasion of an episode, "The First Communion," contained in Féval's book, *The Steps of Conversion*.

Bloy's energetic response could not have entirely pleased Féval, who had become a Christian

---

[16]*La Chevalière de la mort*: see *On The Threshold of the Apocalypse*, wherein Bloy recommends against reading that derivative work.

only recently, and was a very devout one, but who lacked the broadmindedness necessary to understand Catholics of Bloy or Hello's stamp, whose work always remained a dead letter to the good Féval.

The latter writer, the day after reading the famous article by Bloy, wrote to Barbey d'Aurevilly:

> *As for myself, the surprisingly beautiful article did not please me, and you can easily guess why, but it's a Christian of the most eloquent Catholicism, and precisely because of that superior eloquence, who systematically shuts all the doors.*

And imagine Féval's stupefaction when he heard Hello cry out: "We are all going to perish, Bloy alone will remain!"

With Léon Bloy not having written anything yet of importance, Ernest Hello's expostulation seemed too very like an unintelligible prophesy to Féval, who saw in Hello only the unfortunately too certain ridiculousness of his attitude.

"His weeping hair," wrote Féval referring to Hello, "have the same effect on me as if they were found in a soup made of his sobbed glory..."

As for Barbey d'Aurevilly, he stopped his exhortations [to Bloy] only to replace them with advice:

"A person should not read authors too similar

to himself," he wrote,[17] "he should read those who are different. Read Voltaire, read something lighter..."

Despite his confidence in Barbey d'Aurevilly, Léon Bloy must never have followed that advice of reading Voltaire, who seemed to him, and had always seemed to him, rather heavy.

But let's get back to that year of 1879, when Barbey d'Aurevilly undertook to introduce Bloy to his friend from Saint-Sauveur, the abbot Anger. He communicated to him one or more issues of the *Foyer*, a small and virtuous hebdomadary journal whose editor was Charles Buet, a journalist of some talent, who mixed from time to time with the literary group in question.

Léon Bloy had published several articles in the *Foyer*. The article communicated by Barbey to the abbot Anger was entitled *la Maison-Dieu*,[18] and it is made up of two rather copious chapters on the Trappist monastery. Eight years later, they were included in *The Desperate Man*.

The abbot Anger wrote immediately thereafter to Barbey d'Aurevilly:

February 4, 1879.

Very dear Master,

I hold the Foyer *in my claws, and under my eyes of a lynx, all has been*

---

[17]Original footnote: Letters to Léon Bloy, I V., *Mercure de France*.

[18]la Maison-Dieu: La Trappe Abbey, or La Grande Trappe.

*read, devoured with fine teeth, imme-
diately on receipt. As at Domfront, city
of grief, no sooner arrived than
hanged. Justly, it is the happy land of
dom M. the minister, although noble.
He is a shame to his caste.*

*... Léon Bloy is in my opinion a liter-
ary lion, a writer of race, a man of
your dynasty, of your blood. He really
has all the earmarks of genius: always
to the bottom of things and coming
back up to the surface, full of lights,
colors, with outpourings that expand
at the end of his periods like the ex-
pected bouquet, presaged, of a fire-
work. He has a force, a view of things,
a language all his own. Assuredly that
man belongs to your school and your
high lineage. Yes, to be sure, you in-
sufflated him with your spirit, your I-
don't-know-what that he made his own
as all men of genius know how to do.
Beside you, old lion of Atlas, Bloy is
still merely a cub,* sed crescit in
leonem miræ tuæ magnitudinis! *He is
fully provisioned with the instrument
of Reason, he has the auger that taps
the artesian well of truth.*

*He has the just, clear, marked design
that is clearly distinguishable under
the shading, stumping, and hachures*

of his imagination. And that easily-moved heart of his has electric heat, which always, in the evening, brings on the lightning and the thunder, slowly forged in the fire of a midday sun.

I do not speak of his feelings of sanctity which are like the atmosphere of his letters.

One sees quite clearly that he has been struck, that he has the sickness of the other world, and that he begins to suffer in our land of the dead.

That complete harmony of the soul is rare, very rare: genius and sanctity in the same being.

And it is you who, with your thunderbolts, staggered him while he was on his way to Damascus.[19] What merit, what power to tame such men and attach them to oneself like subdued lions!

Farewell! illustrious Tamer. Sleep well on your bed of glory. After such conquests, God ought to be content with you. Ask him for the strength, from the God of the Strong, in the name of the marked exploits that you have effected for his benefit. It is the

---

[19] ... on his way to Damascus: a reference to St. Paul and his conversion.

foremost of all services that you could render Him, and given He is an equitable King and the perfect appreciator of services rendered, He cannot but grant your request which, besides, He orders that all men do for Him.

Do not take too long to write me again, my gulf is open and longs for prey like a Norwegian Maelstrom.

A thousand thanks.

— ANGER.

And several days later, he wrote to Léon Bloy himself, as follows:

February 25, 1879.

Very dear Sir,

Yesterday I received your letter and a copy of the Foyer *containing your article on enthusiasm. Yes, you are precisely that* madman *whom I love, whom I admire, and whom I'm mad about myself. You are persuaded that I was mistaken about your moral and literary worth, in my letter to M. d'Aurevilly. Believe whatever you wish, my dear madman, but I maintain everything I said and what's more listen up: after your letter and the four pages on enthusiasm, I confirm my affirmations and I declare you to be touched like some Rare people whom we have in France of that spirit of sublime dementia who made the crazy David dance before the ark, while he clearly saw that his wife and all his court mocked him. He danced all the same, harp in hand. He was an enthusiast, a character in the midst of the drips, fops, and wet hens who composed his noble and pitiable entourage.*

Do not be discouraged, a man of your stamp will always have his day of legitimate glory.

I had got wind of the Paul Féval affair, but I didn't know that it was that hideous on the part of the pious boutique. Oh! how these Catholics mad for money do us so much ill! What a void of virtues, what speculations by famished misers, under the mask of hypocritical piety! I am familiar with such pious bookstores that make me hate all that throng of deceitful people.

I am of course very happy to see the history of Saint Radegund in your hands.

Leave everything to Providence. Once you have set out, you must wait unper-

turbedly for the effect, and whatever it might be do not succumb to discouragement in the case of failure, nor lose yourself in exultation in the event of success. It is in this equilibrium that strength resides.

You will make me very happy to advise me of the response by Mgr. Pie, if you don't mind.

Your letter, which I have before my eyes, is admirable. It shows to me your entire soul, not your talent, nor your views only, nor your warmth of feeling, but your entire soul, that is to say the totality of your person.

I have a strong desire to know you. I entreat you instantly to send me your photograph so that I can see in what house you lodge: the house always has a bit of the attitude of the person inside. I beseech you to tell me your story in four pages.

I would like to know where you see yourself in the future, for, whatever the career that you launch yourself into, you are one of those who leave a deep and brilliant imprint. There are men who, in good or in evil, cannot be mediocre! You have the three great faculties that make a man A MAN: the rage for exploration of an idea, an opulent imagination whose gourmand branches I will prune, and that warmth of soul and heart that fulfills your edifice and makes you decidedly a madman, *by which I mean very wise.*

Is your body in as good a shape as your mind?

Farewell! I wait to hear from you...

— ANGER.

In the letter that follows, we will see that Léon Bloy had begun his works of exegesis with respect to the beatification of Christopher Columbus. That work was the foundation of his first book, *The Revealer of the Globe*, which didn't appear until 1884, for it is only in that epoch, once again, that Léon Bloy began to gain the necessary confidence in himself.

March 25, 1879.

Very dear Monsieur,

I am very grateful to you for having sent to me a copy of your article on the Beatification of Christopher Columbus. No more there than anywhere else, your talent and the warmth of your faith do not abandon you. You work with a brilliance at the divulgation of a great cause and you will discover in turn, for the world, a great man, a great saint, which is equal in value to a world. That would be a misfortune if your quill should not be consecrated entirely and constantly in the service of the Church. You are a writer of race and a sincere thinker, deep and original in a frivolous and deceitful century. How is it possible that our illustrious friend, today dean of French genius, had not touched the story of Christopher Columbus? I have been tormenting him for two months now that he might treat us to Vauban! For certain men, one needs a man. And you, my dear friend, you are a man capable of taking the measure of certain men with your quill.

I had asked for a Epitome historiæ tuæ[20] *and your photograph. I put great stock in those 2 things.*

Included is the price for the Revue; a thousand thanks.

– ANGER.

The correspondence between abbot Anger and Léon Bloy had been established:

July 23, 1879.

Very dear Sir,

---

[20]*Epitome...*: Latin for "a summary of your history" or background.

I just received M. d'Aurevilly's article from the fifteenth. If you don't mind passing that information on to him for me, I am afraid he'll be absent from Paris by the time my letter arrives. The criticism is worthy of Chateaubriand; the great writer's ghost shivers on finding a kindred talent to speak well of him. I am writing from bed, with much pain. My letter for Palmé is all set in my head. I have only to cast it into the mold of expression, when I can get around to it.

Chin up, your day will come!

Your article, although fallen on deaf ears, says quite often that it is still you.

Bye for now.

— ANGER.

October 30, 1879

Very dear Monsieur Bloy,

I received your sad letter like a chapter out of Jeremiah. Dear friend, you must believe in yourself: you carry in all your soul, not in a small corner of it, enough elements to say to the future: "you are mine!" The more that future is bound to be beautiful and durable, the harder and bloodier it will be to lay the groundworks for it. Every man of your same fiber, who is bound one day to have his glory, resembles Hannibal, who had purchased a battlefield at the price of two thirds of his army and the best of his two eyes.

I myself know, dear friend, the taste of the absinthe that you drink.

Yes, I pray for you. Do not grow upset with the minutes that pass too slowly because they are bitter. God treats you like one of the strong.

— ANGER.

The following letter is dated 1882. As one can see, by what follows, in the letter to O. Mirbeau, to which one must always return, it is the date of the unspeakable catastrophe that precipitated Léon Bloy into literary life. The abbot Anger will more than ever join together with Barbey d'Aurevilly in inducing their friend to begin work. He writes to him about an article:

O.-L. of Deliverance. – February 23, 1882

Very dear Monsieur Bloy,

You do better than O.S. who does not

*come back to life except after Lent.
You, you come back to life beforehand.*

*One always has a great love for those
who are in advance; your ideas are so
suited to you and your style as well,
that the excellent article of our illustrious master on Marcus Aurelius and
which I still have before my eyes, did
not prevent me from seeing the real
beauties of yours. In the order of the
mind, you are clearly of the race of
nobles from the country of the mind.
The mind is my very deep way of referring to the soul and the genius that it
is the shining sheath of.*

*The illustrious [master] must be con-
tent to see his disciple turning out so
well; but, in my opinion, the disciple
too often lets his quill collect dust,
which quill would rather wish to be
active. Why then, dear talent, do you
write so little? Your quill should always be in your hand. I am very grateful to you, and I entreat you to believe
in all my respectful affection.*

— ANGER.

Then all of a sudden the abbot becomes frightened,
the future author of *The Desperate Man* let out a cry
of sorrow and rage.

March 4, 1882.

Very dear Monsieur Bloy,

You are not a man, but a volcano of activity, heated by I do not know how many atmospheres. It is true, you are famished for the absolute, *but be careful of that incandescent lava. Between the burning walls of your brain, fires have shot up which you must subjugate like boiling mists of vapor to the economic laws that render them serviceable and not destructible. The art of governing oneself and governing the physical and mental forces of this world are resolved quite simply in the royalty of man. Here below, among men, none of our forces, at the risk of breaking us pointlessly and breaking others, cannot be abandoned to its blind ardors. The* Modus *is reason's great dogma. One must take the world such as it is, man does not resemble heaven, he does not explode in violence, but with that divine slowness that is a visible law of nature and that God seems to have imposed on himself as he created worlds and organized our planet. Wisdom, the first of all wisdoms, after that of virtue, is discovering in this universal chaos the very real and very distinct laws that, in their harmony, found the entire order in us, and outside of us. Be careful of the absolute, it is a sun that could burn your eyes! Only God has the absolute attributes that we apperceive through distant infinities and which our reason is the pale and enfeebled reflection of. If you want to concentrate those divine fires on the disk of your soul, like the lens that a physician uses to focus scattered rays on a point, the eye of your soul, too unequal to the fury of that flame of the absolute, will die extinguished and consumed.*

In spite of everything, there are still thousands of Saints!

Keep your eyes wide open in that Paris of yours! Study well in the Gospel O. S. J.-C. To know how to attain the degree that he got to, to know like him how to deal with men suaviter et fortiter, *that there is the masterwork of human schemes!*

Goodbye for now, and a thousand thank you's for your complete confidence.

– ANGER.

Léon Bloy however began, with his first published articles, that war on the mediocre and lukewarm clergy, a war lasting thirty years before long, whose attacks were not always without effect. That's the abbot

Anger's opinion, as one will see:

> *Our Lady of Deliverance. – March 10, 1882.*
>
> *Very dear Monsieur Bloy,*
>
> *Your new* Pensum *has greatly intrigued me. I have felt the blows of your whip disarmed of spikes and nails in order to spare your sacred name and avoid scandals. But for those who know how to read between the lines and read your intentions, under the profundity of your diaphanous expressions, one sees that you suffer from our sacerdotal tepidity which makes great souls suffer enormously. We greatly deserve that* pensum *that ought to revive us, but Priests do not read the* Foyer. *Your clamors of Isaac ought to resound on the heights of all the great papers of the Press which fall each morning down to the masses from that high Paris whence good and evil rush in avalanches over all of France.*
>
> *So choose better then, the place that you will speak from. We all have need of sincere and bold teachings.*
>
> *We others,* Preachers, *we have need of a good jab.*

The so very strong bullocks of our plains, who pull heavy carts with so vigorous and so gentle a pace, fall asleep standing up and nod off in the monotony of their walking even. The herdsman awakens them when they lie down with the proud blow of his iron-clad stick on their crupper or along the small of their back.

So too with us, the bullocks of the good God, who work the fallow soil of this world, we are somnolent, the blow displeases us and makes us bellow. Dear herdsman, strikes us all the same rhythmically on our good back, for our master wants his steer to work wide furrows and the days to be good.

Goodbye for now, and a thousand thank you's for your good stick as well.

— ANGER.

January 11, 1884.

Very dear friend,

Doubtless it was you yourself who sent me the day before yesterday the two articles by M. d'Aurevilly on Labre and the Curate d'Ars! It has all the earmarks of a friendly hand! I savored those two morsels, immersed in a sort of inebriation of the heart and spirit. However, the master left me my part to play on the same subject, but in the way he takes his hero, he leaves nothing to say to even the strongest of men, who might wish to treat of that same subject.

With the back of the pen, he sends recoiling, out of commission, that poor little tommy of Aubineau, who dared collect in an insipid little book the immense poverty of that sublime and royal poor man. Goodbye, dear Monsieur, chin up, our day will come sooner or later. Remember that I suffer as much as you do, but we will be victorious together.

— ANGER.

The first book by Léon Bloy, *The Revealer of the Globe*, was about to appear; it is the subject of the following letters:

February 5, 1884.

Very dear friend,

I did receive your beautiful volume on Christopher Columbus with your very friendly envoi by the author. I have cast a quick glance here and there at your work. Your ideas please to no end my spirit and enflame my heart for the book's hero and author. I'm not quite myself yet. I need to read with a clear head and from one end to the other of your eloquent study, and then I will take pen in hand and open the gates of my soul widely to let out warm effusions. What a shame that our souls operate at the same diapason and that we are located so infinitely distant from each other.

Yes, of course, I include you in my prayers and I ask that you to do the same. A thousand times thank you, and until we speak again, soon.

— ANGER.

Saint-Sauveur-le-Vicomte. — May 7, '84.

Very dear Monsieur,

I have read your beautiful book from cover to cover!

It is really a work by the hand of a master, but by a master in burning contradiction to the spirit of this miserable and abased century! Mgr. the Bishop of Coutances, to whom I have made your work amply known, is of my same opinion, but His Greatness knows only how to groan, and groan is all he can do, in the face of the preponderant obstacles that have stopped the good Catholic movement in favor of the canonization of Ch. Columbus! I was thinking to see Mgr. the Bishop of Nantes as well, but he did not come; I expect another opportunity to meet with His Greatness about the goal that your work proposes to attain. The most that I can do is a very succinct analysis of your book, which I will have inserted into two or three diocesan Catholic reviews, which are read only, alas! by poor curates and some good women who will be of no assistance.

There is no enthusiasm anymore that we are aware of: that divine thing is dead and me who am a bit ardent, I pass before the eyes of our ice-cold people for a fanatic, a nut, a good-for-nothing.

Our so-called Catholics hold virtues in horror; in the place of devotion, they want nothing anymore than the insipid and somniferous devotions compatible with an oblivion of all the sacrifices that are demanded by the situation we find ourselves in.

Politics cannot count on them any more than religion can.

Where then is the courage and the strength of those lions nourished by J.-C. and the Holy Spirit that J. Chrysostome speaks about? Ah! dear friend, we are bound to grow desperate like Jeremiah over the moral ruins that the Revolution created. There are no more souls anymore, there are no more men!

What we need is for God to come, lightning in hand: the duel will be visible and frightening. I do not believe that God has been seized by the collar yet as he will do in short order with the rebels of the earth. Everything is ripe. I do not believe that the signal for battle is too far off. It will be an appalling save-yourself-if-you-can, but who will ever be able to escape the blows of a vengeance whose angers have been collecting for hundreds of years on top of these impious generations!

Ah! dear friend, would that I could live in your company or in your vicinity. My saddened soul would have need of the human and superhuman

*strength that one finds in conversation
with a determined Christian like yourself. I remain alone with God!*

*Please believe me, dear friend, when I
say that I live with you in thought and
that I am happy to know that you are
praying for me.*

– ANGER.

One may conclude by these appreciations and by
these encouragements that Léon Bloy's genius as a
writer already appeared in the writings to which he attached little importance; one may also say that abbot
Anger was gifted with a certain critical sensibility and
a wonderful enthusiasm.

But the ignorance that all Léon Bloy's friends
were in, at that time, as to what his interior existence
was like, did not permit them to guess at his true nature. When *The Desperate Man* came out, everyone
wanted to know that book and all they got out of it
was the violence. From that moment forward, the author became a lambasting pamphleteer, exclusively.

Very few understood that the aggressive and
brutal form was, for Léon Bloy, merely a cuirass. He
saw himself surrounded by enemies from the get-go,
because he was a Christian, and he made it a necessity to be redoubtable.

In examining the thirty volumes – I do not
count the brochures – that form today his complete
body of work, one is struck above all by the incredi-

ble variety of that work wherein lambast holds but a very small place since *The Desperate Man*, in which already there were other things than just lambast.

Salvation Through the Jews, that masterpiece that has so much difficulty being known as it would need to be known, appears to me the most perfect example of the books ideated by the author. That book is really the result of the interior Peace that I spoke of earlier, it is truly the expression of that permanent contemplation and of that intense tenderness that composed Léon Bloy's true basis.

I will add that there are, in all his other books, pages made similarly and fetched from the same source. One discovers them from the very beginnings of Léon Bloy, in 1881, at the *Chat Noir* journal, and at the *Figaro*. One will discover them more than ever in his correspondences, which we will see soon enough.

For all that, no works of youth, no imitations either. One could cite, at a pinch, *la Chevalière de la Mort*, in which the memory of a reading of Carlyle by the author is apparent and the first short story in the volume *Sueur de Sang*, entitled "The Abyssinian," in which Barbey d'Aurevilly's style can be recognized. From the first day he began writing, Léon Bloy was the original and powerful writer that he was to the very end.

Trip to Denmark

When Léon Bloy, in June 1900, undertook to recount the seventeen months that he had spent in Denmark, he made no mention of the first time he had sojourned in that country, in 1891.

One can have no inkling then, when reading *Seventeen Months in Denmark*, that Bloy had found some pleasure in that small realm. That was the case, however, for reasons that I want to talk about; and the letter that follows, addressed to M. Georges Landry, will serve as a witness to support my argument:

> *Bagsværd by Lyngby (Denmark), February 26, '91.*
>
> *Dear friend,*
>
> *... You must have felt that something strangely decisive was happening to me. Imagine me at an enormous distance from Paris and from France, where I live with my wife and at my mother-in-law's, as if in a dream, in the hinterland of a very solitary country, peopled principally by countless crows that hold council in the vicinity of the house, close enough to wake me at night.*
>
> *Rollinat would not fail to imagine fantastic things here. There is simply much cold and much melancholy. I*

feel so far from everything, even from Copenhagen, which is a center after all and a large city where I felt nearly desperate. I cannot learn a single word of the language, and I would not dare take a step outside without someone's assistance. Even the food disconcerts me at time. Truth be told, many people understand a little bit of French and an evident sympathy welcomes all French people in this country.

But I am a solitary here until the day I might climb up onto the stage as a lecturer. For you have guessed it doubtless, I have no other part to play.

... I am told that a certain success due to curiosity is not impossible, and I was able to observe by my own eyes the avidity, more or less intelligent, of the public for all things French.

I was in Copenhagen the day before yesterday with my wife. We had gone to the Catholic church to hear a Dominican who is talked about by the people. People go to see his white robes which are, in this country, a sort of marvel, and one gives the impression of knowing French – which passes for being infinitely distinguished. If these Protestants understood exactly

*what this Father utters to them, it is
probable that his popularity would
wane. The good people cannot believe
that they are in the presence of a
Catholic priest come boldly to confess
his faith. But, it is nothing of the sort.
That Dominican deceives them and
robs them ignobly. He speaks to them
of Renan, of Science, of evangelical
documents, of the existence of God,
etc... You see that. Not a word of the
Church, nor of the Saints, nor of
Mary. Nothing, except the robe, which
could make one doubt that one is in
the presence of a real priest. It's the
politics of cowardice. The wretch was
ashamed of Jesus Christ. We were suf-
focating with disgust and indignation
to see ourselves represented thus and
left before the end, at the risk of upset-
ting everyone who was there. I had immediately resolved to send, the following day, as a Catholic, a protestation
to the principle journals of Copenhagen. I renounced the idea realizing
that it would be terrible for my conscience to distance in that way several
souls whom the imbecilic words of that
religious, all the same, bring together
at the foot of the altar.*

*But I saw, on that occasion, the cer-
tain prestige that yammering on in*

French holds. I will take advantage of it then, if it please God. I know contemporary literature rather well, and I have with me a complete copy of Belluaires et Porchers. *I will serve that up to them as properly as I can. Perhaps I will obtain enough success to gain an honest sum.*

Until then, I vegetate in the countryside, with the regret of being here in this season. In the summer, it must be marvelous. At two paces away from my lodging, the woods begin, and what woods! my friend! Pines and small lakes with no end in sight. A Finland in miniature. My only recourse at the present moment is to wander there, in the afternoons, despite the cold and ice. God knows whether I'll be given the opportunity to see these charming woods again under better conditions.

Finally, I am a little down, but not devastated! I wait, as always, for God to give me some place in this world where clearly he has not cast me only to make me suffer without purpose.

I thank you for having sent me the first installments of Là-bas. *I am impatient to read what follows.*

I am going to send to Deschamps[21] a study on the book by Hérisson.[22] I think that you regularly receive La Plume... *I cannot think of any errands I could ply you with. That will come doubtless, if my sojourn here should be prolonged. While waiting, I embrace you.*

Yours,

– LÉON BLOY.

P.S. – A last request. Write to me, even if just a few lines. I do not expect that you will do it. I want to refrain from hoping. But I think that would be an act of mercy. You were far from France once and a captive. You know what a letter means then, even if banal.

I do not want to end this letter without returning to that impression of minor sadness that I spoke of and which is, in short, more superficial than profound.

My wife's family is immensely sweet and tender. They are a thousand leagues away from supposing me to be a man of little importance or a Bo-

---

[21]Original footnote: Léon Deschamps, then director of *La Plume*.

[22]Original footnote: *La légende de Metz*.

> *hemian like certain people in Paris*
> *have the goodness to suppose. I am*
> *profoundly respected here and perfect-*
> *ly loved. They know me to be poor*
> *and, thus far, unsuccessful, but as they*
> *know the real reasons for all that and*
> *because they understand them ad-*
> *mirably, they esteem me all the more,*
> *and they are persuaded that the future*
> *will treat me as I deserve.*
>
> *So, no sadness from that quarter then,*
> *– quite the contrary.*
>
> *If Paris was not so far away, my joy*
> *would be perfect. My wife asks me to*
> *send you her most affectionate "bon-*
> *jour."*

Léon Bloy was married in May, 1890 and several
months later, he had resolved with Mme. Bloy to try
living in Denmark. They departed in the month of
February, 1891. Their sojourn was eight months long;
their oldest daughter Véronique Bloy was born in
Bagsværd.

The welcome they received by the Molbech
family facilitated Léon Bloy's first contact with Denmark. And yet the family comprised only three people
then, Mme. Molbech and her daughters.

The son had expatriated several years earlier
and was living in America. Léon Bloy was unable to
meet him until ten years later.

As for the father, the poet Christian Molbech, he had died a short time before his daughter and Léon Bloy were engaged.

One can only regret the absence of relations between him and his father-in-law who spoke French and understood its beauty.

Christian Molbech had been a man with a keen mind, very open and even rather biting wit. He is above all famous in Denmark for his dramatic works, the main one of which is *Ambroise*, which is put on from time to time in Copenhagen and always with success. *Ambroise* is a drama or rather a comedy-drama which, when read, makes one think of certain pieces by Alfred de Musset.

Grotesques, as with the poet of *On ne badine pas...* come and go without suspecting the terrible battle endured by the young secretary-poet and the girl who has fallen in love with him. A brutally honest play wherein one need not search for the ambitions of a Julien Sorel any more than the liberties of the *Chandelier*.

It has been translated into French, but it has never been performed in France where it would have perchance a warm reception. I still prefer Christian Molbech's poetry to *Ambroise*. They abound in fresh images, light sketches and fine critiques. It's a treat to hear Mme. Bloy translate them impromptu while emphasizing certain passages that she prefers.

The small town that Léon Bloy inhabited, upon his arrival in Denmark, was, one guessed it from the letter to Georges Landry, near Copenhagen, and Bloy was spot on when he spoke of that Finland in miniature which is, in the summer, marvelous. He was able to contemplate the marvel from the month of May forward, and more then ever he wandered under the trees reciting the Juvenal that he was studying passionately at that time, aloud. The Danish peasants who heard him, nicknamed him "the singing professor."

Under the trees, at fifty meters from their habitation, there was a small hut half-hidden by the branches where, as soon as good weather arrived, Léon Bloy installed himself in order to work, and it was in that rustic pavilion where he wrote the first chapters of *The Woman Who Was Poor*.

The vicinity of Copenhagen, as it turns out, would allow the writer to become a lecturer.

Léon Bloy prepared himself for the task, from the day after his arrival, and the following month, on March 20, a preliminary reading entitled *The Funeral of Naturalism* was given in Sprogforening.

Bloy spoke, on that first evening, before a rather large crowd, but his voice was not very supple and it was a bit too deep, so it did not carry sufficiently. He realized this and corrected his delivery in such a way that he was applauded at subsequent conferences. There were two others, one on Villiers de l'Isle-Adam and another on Baudelaire.

Of all that, we have only the text of the first, published in Copenhagen by the publisher G. E. C.

Gad. It's a small book of twenty-four pages including the title – a simple and amusing bibliographic curiosity because the Léon Bloy hinted at in it is unexpected. One does not easily imagine the ungrateful beggar uttering phrases like the following:

"... Above all I wish to thank you, to render thanks from the bottom of my heart, for the trouble you have taken to come here in such great numbers..."

Or this: "... The Danish have an excellent reputation in Europe. One vaunts, just about everywhere, their gentleness, their extreme politeness, and above all the astonishing culture of their minds..."

Mme. Bloy not having attended those literary soirées, it is unfortunately impossible to reconstruct the two conferences that were left unpublished.

In addition to those visits to Copenhagen, Léon Bloy took advantage of several excursions and one of those merits relating.

The pretext of the trip they made, that day, Mme. Bloy and her husband, was to pay a visit to a relative, a cousin of the Molbech's, who lived with her adopted daughter in a retired corner of the wood.

The husband of that lady, a painter, had died several years earlier, not mad, but a maniac to the point of making believe sometimes in the irremediable loss of his mental balance. He had lived his entire life in the lodging where, for better or worse, rather worse than better, the two women continued to subsist. To visit them, one had to take a long path through the wood; the path was dark and the wood had a dreadful sadness to it. As soon as the visitor caught glimpse of the house, he came upon a well, just in front of his feet, without a wall around it, a horrible black and gaping hole that gave one a tremendous fright.

On the interior of that habitation, a rather spacious room held works by the deceased painter on display, an incalculable number of canvases; the walls were covered with them, all the way up to the ceiling. And all those canvases were invariably blue, a sinister mold-blue color with yellow touches here and there. In a word, they were nightmarish paintings that augmented the feeling of despondency and disturbance that their passage there had given them. Léon Bloy and his wife were received, in any case, warmly by their relative; the old woman explained to them how she lived by means of a small photography business, and Bloy remembered then having remarked, not without stupefaction, a frame filled with portraits on the facade of that strange abode.

On the evening of that visit, after having returned home, Léon Bloy wanted to consign to his journal what he had seen, still distressed by it. As he sat in his small pavilion under the pines, he wrote a gripping narrative that soon turned into a tale entitled "The House of the Devil."

And when, two years later, he was commissioned to providing the *Gils Blas*, regularly, with stories from the war of 1870-71, he had merely to situate his story in the Marne and add to it three Uhlans in order to turn it into one of the most captivating tales in *Sueur de Sang*. As for how exact his description of the place is, it is not impossible, even today, to verify that. The house of the devil still exists, such as it did, and its terrifying well without a wall never fails to frighten visitors by the brusqueness of its appearance, after their having been oppressed by the sad woods they had just traversed.

One can still see on the exterior wall of the edifice, as before, portraits that serve as a kind of advertising, for the inhabitant of the place continues the photography business of the adoptive mother. And it is probable that the walls of the eating room are, as before, filled with the terrifying blue canvases of the unknown painter, who did not, clearly, paint horrors so much as give the author of *Sueur de Sang* the opportunity to write yet another work of art.

Léon Bloy in Lagny

The first time I met Léon Bloy was at the train station in Lagny, in 1901.

We corresponded for several months before that. I was living in Tours; he was residing in Lagny. I had informed him of my intention to visit him and spend a day. He responded to me as follows:

> *Dear friend,*
>
> *My wife and I are overjoyed to hear of your promise to visit. For we want it to be a promise, and we are waiting with impatience to see you.*
>
> *I will wait for you at the train station. You will recognize me by the red book I will be holding in my hand...*

At the train station in Lagny, Léon Bloy was punctual. He was dressed in grey, coiffed in a very stiff brown felt hat which he had difficult time keeping on his head, which was so absolutely round that it made the hat conformer's measurements roundly pointless. He held in his right hand a prayer book that was bound in red shagreen, which he made visible, as he had said he would do.

I approached him: "Léon Bloy?"

He responded: "René Martineau?" Then he put his book in his pocket, and we walked side by side.

My immediate impression was that of a strong and stiff Léon Bloy; an impression that, since then, has been much modified. But it is certain that, at that time, the author of *The Desperate Man* was successful in his practice of presenting a redoubtable external appearance.

His hair was white, but his behavior was not that of an old man. He had a solid and easy air about him.

The portrait of him by Charles Cain, the frontispiece of the first edition of *Sueur de Sang*, produced rather exactly the effect that I am trying to convey. In what followed, Léon Bloy little by little gave the lie to that attitude. In reality, his prodigious physical strength had been fabricated by Rudolphe Salis and augmented by Barbey d'Aurevilly, whom that legend greatly amused.

After *Le Pal*, a journalist said to Barbey: "With lambasts of that sort, your friend Léon Bloy could attract some bad business to himself. It is known that he returns home rather late at night in your deserted neighborhood..."[23]

"Bah!" retorted Barbey. "But... how many are there of you?... Because... if you are twenty or more, I will warn him. But if you are only eight or ten, I'm not worried about it."

---

[23]Original footnote: Léon Bloy resided on rue Rousselet, as did Barbey d'Aurevilly.

During that rather long walk we took, for he lived far from the train station, I tried to penetrate his personal thoughts. What I had read from his books and our recent correspondence helped me with that.

Evidently Léon Bloy was saying to himself: "And here we have yet another person who comes to me! I have a great desire to open my heart to him, but I have suffered so greatly by the abandonment of a large number of friends, that I do not dare, and I would like to test him. Besides, what could I tell him, other than that I'm very unfortunate and miserable!..."

Meanwhile, we had passed the bridge over the Marne and traversed the small valley that separates Pompone from Lagny, ugly and insipid landscape like almost all the countryside around Paris.

We arrived at rue St.-Laurent, as banal a street as they get; Léon Bloy resided at number 9.

He was the neighbor of a locksmith, and with a large gilt key he succeeded in opening the door to the hallway that served as a common entryway to the house.

The apartment was small, but well kept. From the window of the room that he was used to work in, the artist could see trees, which were, throughout his life, indispensable to him: "Without the view of a garden," he told me, "my soul would wither and die of horror," or even: "I have two passions in life, trees and the imperfect subjunctive."

The reception I received by Mme. Bloy, on

rue Saint-Laurent, was extremely cordial and Léon
Bloy, at home, became very expansive: he introduced
me to his children and, during lunch, that man who
has so often been accused of exclusively hateful feelings spoke to me of the several friends that he had,
with tenderness and bonhomie. The name of Alfred
Vallette came often to his lips with regards to his next
book, *l'Exégèse des Lieux communs*, which he said
should garner an exceptional success, the "Mercure"
having consented to the publication of several chapters from it, in its newspaper, before the volume came
out.

For Léon Bloy, like many artists, was only
ever interested in the work he was in the process of
creating and he carried that feeling to the most extreme limits of hope, which turned out to be a cruel
delusion when the book was finally published.

That, however, did not prevent him from getting back to work again with the same consciousness,
and, as the new work came along, his illusions reap-
peared.

He could hardly do otherwise. He felt his
power of realization and then, when he read fragments of the work that he had just finished to his
friends, they were amazed, which electrified him even
more by their bravos.

The number of readers he had acquired, at
least in the second half of his literary career, grew, it
must be said, to considerable proportions; but never
enough to assure him of large print runs that would

have changed his material life by removing all his worries.

Léon Bloy, while speaking to me about that *Exégèse* which cost him so much effort, named several authors that he admired, and I saw, from that first day, what I had often noticed afterwards, that Léon Bloy, the man, was infinitely less severe than Léon Bloy the writer.

He spoke to me with enthusiasm of Villiers de l'Isle-Adam and of Edgar Allan Poe.

The first of these two poets was particularly dear to him, and of all the men of letters that he frequented and frequently read, nobody was more to his liking than Villiers. Léon Bloy spoke of Villiers very often. At first in *Histoires désobligeantes*, where Lazarus is none other than Villiers; then in *The Woman Who Was Poor* with its admirable portrait of Bohémond de l'Isle-de-France whom Bloy lovingly depicted. I told him of my admiration for that capital morsel. "That makes be very happy to hear," he said, "that you saw that. Poor Villiers! It was he whom I had in mind!"

Léon Bloy's conversation was, what is more, exempt of banalities. All the little stories of a small town, all the disputes with the proprietor, the grocer, the baker, or the curate which occupied a large place in his journal at the time when I saw him in Lagny, in 1901, could not be guessed at by listening to him speak, and, until the moment when *Quatre ans de Captivité en Cochons-sur-Marne* came out, I was totally in the dark as to Mme. Tuparle and the abbot Vignoble.

In the afternoon, Léon Bloy read to me some of his *Lieux communs*, then he had me join him for a walk along the banks of the Marne.

On exiting his home, Léon Bloy the refractory appeared again; the ugliness of the villas that appeared along the way gave him a sick feeling at heart which he could do nothing about. The constraint became impossible for him before all those expressions of modern taste, and, for we were at the dawn of the automobile age, our encountering a hideous and noisy machine exasperated him. Sometimes he lowered his eyes to the ground and said: "Ah! my God!" Other times he pointed out with his walking stick the ridiculously masked faces of the drivers and cried out loud enough that they could hear him: "Look at those mugs!"

Those ways of his gave me a feeling of well-being; I found an immense comfort standing beside that exile from another epoch in time. I was upset with myself when I thought that my joy was a result of his suffering; but when I told him my thought, he did not hide his satisfaction, and the more he divined the movement of my soul towards his, the more he smiled, for he was like that, avid for affection. And the evening came to a close very gently... around ten thirty.

The following morning we were at mass at seven o'clock. Bloy had waited for me, for habitually he rose at five o'clock in the morning and went to church before the first mass.

I saw him following the mass that day as I saw him do ever since. He had a small book that he recurred to scrupulously, pronouncing the liturgical words at the very moment when the officiant and the acolyte pronounced them.

He took communion. The mass terminated, he made a small sign of grace, stood up and said to me very simply: "We can leave whenever you're ready."

Several hours later, I quit Lagny. Before my departure, Léon Bloy ladened me with his gifts, seeking from among his books and his papers something he knew ought to please me. In this way, he dedicated a photography of himself to me: "Léon Bloy at the time of *The Desperate Man*. It appears that I was as handsome as all that!"

And in the wagon that carried me back to Paris I said to myself: "Thus far, I do not see any trace of his ingratitude."

I had seen, in sum, a proud artist, a believer, a sincere person who did not want to belong to any group, because he felt in himself the strength to think and to work without the aid of paid applause.

His very salutary home consoled him for the hideous things that he was obliged to endure in the outside world.

He considered it with indifference that he had

been made to beg, as the works of art that he had written did not sell. As a Christian, he was honored even to find himself in such a position amidst the idolators of the golden calf.

Not only had Léon Bloy always retained that independence of spirit, but it would have been impossible to deliver him of it. It was a part and parcel of his genius.

Since that first visit that I paid him in Lagny, I saw him grow old, I saw his lassitude for things augment and his anger even calm down; but never did I see him compromise, were it even an inch, the liberty of his judgments or his actions.

What some call his "false judgments" were nothing but the result of a superb indifference for everything that did not have the strength to captivate him.

As for his ingratitude, it was merely a very conscious and resolute determination not to pay for a benefit with a concession. He very often added to that another determination, no less resolute than the first, not to put up with someone who annoyed him, above all by discussions or considerations too foreign to his own ideas which, moreover, he did not impose in any case.

In August 1901, three months after my trip to Lagny, I invited Léon Bloy and his family to sojourn with me in Pouliguen for several weeks.

Bloy related in his journal that little holiday

which he resigned himself to, despite his horror of travel, being desirous to procure for his family a small diversion to the boredoms of Lagny.

Our correspondence on that subject was composed mostly of his hesitations and my insistences.

I suspected the pleasure that my invitation had caused Mme. Bloy and her two children, but I could not imagine the fright with which Léon Bloy envisaged such a trip.

In his letters, he came up with all sorts of difficulties to which "... had been added," he wrote, "the new shame for me of having to request information at a guichet about tickets for bathing..."

That magnification of inconveniences hounded him until he had arrived; he succeeded rather often in communicating it to his family, and he was capable, after an easy trajectory of short duration, to say to me, as if it were the most natural thing in the world, that "We have suffered in the most atrocious way!"

One might have said that the simplest of bothersome events had suddenly put before his eyes something like the synthesis of all the sorrows he had previously endured.

All his person then became menacing and the excess of his lamentations did not calm down until he had resumed his regular habits.

On the day after his arrival in Pouliguen, Léon Bloy planned his days, according to the program that he had been accustomed to follow at home. Out of bed at five o'clock in the morning, he made his way to church at a little before six o'clock, and attended three masses. We joined him at the time of the second mass so as to return to the chalet at Saint-Roch a little before him.

He returned towards eight o'clock in the morning, presented himself at the window of the eating room where we all knew to gather, and said to us with his best smile: "Bonjour!"

He renewed that entrance each morning, with that invariability in the smallest of details of his ordinary life, which one must not frustrate under pain of saddening him or displeasing him.

It is in this way that holidays greatly frightened Léon Bloy by their unexpectedness and also by the momentary rupture to his daily habits.

After breakfast, we took a walk along the roads least traveled.

In the afternoon, Bloy took a half-hour nap, then he resumed his work for two or three hours, after which he consented to read to us several unpublished pages. The evening was spent chatting, unless Bloy played a game of dominos with his oldest daughter.

He recounted in his journal the very nice impression that staying in the vicinity of the small chapel dedicated to Sainte-Anne and Saint-René made on him, which he alludes to in his dedication to *Exégèse des Lieux communs.*

Those who would like to find, today, vestiges of that vacation resort ought to go to Pen-Château, a kind of faubourg of Pouliguen, located in the direction of Grande-Côte. The chapel Sainte-Anne and Saint-René, which could have been seen from the sea formerly, was already thoroughly surrounded by buildings in 1901.

Today, it is on the edge of a veritable street; the only thing conserved is, in front of the principal entrance, a square with the old and curious Calvary that Léon Bloy spoke of.

Trees have been planted on the square. On the opposite side of the chapel, less than one hundred meters away, one will find the chalet de Ker Saint-Roch, but modified and enlarged since the time of Léon Bloy's stay there, to the point of being unrecognizable.

Finally, the entire coast, very exposed at that time, is now occupied by numerous villas. From the windows to the west of the chalet, it is probable that one can no longer see the sea, as one could do formerly, and which Léon Bloy spoke about somewhat in his journal, wherein he notes that he saw the Ocean for the first time in his life: "What do you want," he said to me, "I'm a sylvan, I love above all the trees and the beasts of the forest. The sea, it is very beautiful, but I do not know why I sense an enemy in it that wants to swallow me."

I told him that it was not impossible to find along the Ocean a pleasure analogous to what the forest might offer; and at low tide I led him across the rocks and tufts of sea wrack, into the Grande-Côte grottoes, pointing out to him the peculiarities of the crabs evolving in pools of water.

He murmured, "Yes, it is interesting, your path where there is neither villas nor automobiles."

With his lorgnon on his nose, he looked attentively at the pebbles and discovered in this way, to his stupefaction and my own, for I did not know him as a geologist at this time, a piece of basalt, a rather rare thing in those parts.

One day of high tide, he came and sat down on the top of a rock and remained there for two hours looking at and listening to the waves crashing.

On returning, he said to me: "It's curious, I cannot stop thinking of Hugo and at the quantity of beautiful images he found... When that man pontificates, when he dogmatizes, he's a huge imbecile. But he found images, that much is certain, and looking at the furious sea, I was thinking of him."

At another time, we were on the Pouliguen jetty at the hour when a crowd of bathers were milling about. The temperature was exquisite; the sea was calm; one heard the joyful cries of the children on the beach; the multicolor sail boats were returning to port. Léon Bloy did what he could to enjoy the scene before his eyes; but it was impossible for him not to hear the Naturalistic conversations of our neighbors, and his patience was quickly exhausted; he brusquely surprised the group of bathers, saying loudly and in a gruff tone: "Those people are stupid!" And turning around, he walked back to the port.

At the entrance to the jetty, there is a tall wooden cross and on a pedestal of the cross there is an inscription that asks for prayers for mariners.

On seeing the inscription, Léon Bloy stopped, as if he had discovered suddenly the only reason for his presence in that place, made a big sign of the cross and recited in a firm voice a *Pater* and an *Ave*. Then he distanced himself, indifferent to all that did not concern eternal life.

This anecdote paints a rather complete picture of him: incapable of any restraint that might soften his horror of social contact, turning his back on a scene of beauty in order to shout out his contempt at people, and curbed only by the necessity of praying to God.

As soon as he was alone with me, his humor changed; he forgot what had exasperated him until the next encounter outraging his ideal.

While still in Pouliguen, we made, together with the rest of Bloy's family, several excursions in the region. Our trip to Guérande had immensely pleased Léon Bloy, who wrote about it in his journal:

> ... *For the first time, I see a entirely fortified city, as in the XVth century. The celebrated novel by Balzac stands out vividly in my mind, while I contemplate that adorable vestige... I see the*

du Guénic again, Mlle. des Touches,
and Claude Vignon; I see above all
the detestable Béatrix, and once again
I have that grandiose sensation of the
Nothingness of everything that is visi-
ble and which continually disengages
itself from the immense "Comédie hu-
maine."

The return to Lagny, on August 29, was sad because Léon Bloy's resources were nil and his book, *Exégèse des Lieux communs,* was coming along painfully.

It did not appear until the month of June of the following year (1902).

I have already spoken of the bitterness that the insuccess of his books caused him. Never was the feeling more profound or justified than on the appearance of that *Exégèse* which nobody understood as it deserved to be.

Impossible to find the counterpart of a like work that is both tragic and amusing at the same time, when it isn't a marvel of psychology.

Villiers de l'Isle-Adam and Ernest Hello, cited frequently by Léon Bloy in his *Exégèse,* can be compared to him insofar as irony is concerned.

But Hello was unaware of, and did not write, the kind of Aristophanes-like or Rabelaisian insistence that brings those divers tableaux together in the same frame.

Villiers, lighter, more nervous, more impro-
vising than Léon Bloy, remains ofttimes obscure.

Léon Bloy presses further, imagines a tale
with more difficulty, but he is surprising in clarity, in
spite of the refinements and the continual and voluntary dispersion[24] of his dazzling form.

He knows how to give to the most ordinary of
subjects, as well as to the most preposterous of things,
an unforgettable literary color.

It is enough to ask oneself whether the constancy of that splendid form is not the unique and veritable cause of *Exégèse*'s insuccess.

It is in any case evident that that insuccess
was complete and that the author suffered greatly because of it.

On the copy that he gave me, beside the nicely
printed dedication, he added these words: "Wealth, it
is God the Father, Poverty, it is Jesus, Misery, it is
Love." At the same time, he wrote to me, saying "Do
not speak to me anymore about this book..."

He himself however often spoke to me about
it; on my last visit to Lagny, in February 1904, he
again spoke to me about it.

Léon Bloy no longer lived on rue Saint-Laurent. He had rented a pavilion in a garden.

The garden had charmed him, the lodging was

---

[24]dispersion: in the optical sense of the word, continuing the
metaphor of the refraction of light, or clarity.

inconvenient and poorly maintained.

The quarrels of the renter with the proprietor, – whom he called Mme. Corbillard, – have been recorded in *Quatre ans de Captivité à Cochons-sur-Marne* in a scrupulous manner and give an extremely exact idea of the inconveniences of the structure.

One can read on page 457:

Agonizing with ill-humor, suffocated by indignation, I go to speak with a person already spoken to [by the proprietor presumably], *the bailiff B., in whom I had had the unbelievable surprise of finding a reader of my books and a friend. He shows interest in my situation, promises to see the object of my grievances, and expects to obtain a delay...*

It is in the midst of these anguishments that I found Léon Bloy and found him also precisely when the bailiff B. was visiting, who came generously to offer his services and succeeded, several days later, in preventing his immediate eviction. He had read *The Ungrateful Beggar* and Bloy had secured an ineluctable admiration from that good fellow for everything that the author of the *Beggar* had written.

"Seeing as you do not have *Exégèse,* allow me to offer you a copy, you will be greatly amused. I will read for you, while waiting, one or two chapters which will give you the tone of the book." And Bloy opened his copy and began reading, standing right in front of his attentive listener.

I will never be able to forget the stupefaction painted on the face of that ministerial officer, from the first phrases.

Léon Bloy had chosen the story entitled: "Health above all!"

The stupefaction soon turned into stupor when Bloy got to the last paragraph: "Know this, my friends, that I have never sold anything but [shit]...!" The bailiff stood up appalled and was not really reassured until he saw us, Mme. Bloy and myself, laughing openly, as much at the look on his face as at what he had heard.

Bloy began laughing too, finished reading, and then repeated: "You'll be greatly amused."

And I don't tell this anecdote merely for the amusement we obtained by a great artist's interlocutor, who was easily disconcerted, but to tell of Bloy's amiability and warm-heartedness towards a man whom he suspected of only admiration and generosity towards him, his good humor in spite of the anguishment that was torturing him.

In 1903, while Léon Bloy was still living at Lagny, the following book appeared: *The Last Columns of the Church*.

The author of that book returned to lambast, whose form it seems he had wanted to rejuvenate. These are not the vigorous portraits of personalities,

as found in *The Desperate Man* or *Le Pal*, but carica-
tures of their works. Léon Bloy choosing ridiculous
morsels and weak passages as examples.

The Reverend P. Judas, written twelve years
before the other chapters, is certainly the best of that
work, which ends with *The Last Catholic Poet*, a bold
and curious criticism wherein Léon Bloy shows his
enthusiasm for the very great and extremely singular
poet who is Jehan Rictus. Everyone has read the *Soliloquies du Pauvre*, a poignant book, of intense poetry, with an abundance of very new images to ravish
the author of *The Woman Who Was Poor*. Jehan Rictus speaks in slang and writes it as he speaks it, using
apocope in a methodical and frequent way.

Léon Bloy having remarked to him that his
poetry would gain by being written in a stricter format, the author of *Soliloquies* responded to him by a
letter which is, in my eyes, one of the most profound
and clearest literary pages of our times.

That admirable letter had moreover the result
of completely convincing Léon Bloy, who inserted it
in his book and added these words to it: "... not a single atom of my objections remain. I have finally understood! Rictus' slang, I espouse it amorously from
here on out..."

Thus have I always seen Léon Bloy, lacking
in a rigid thinking and prejudice, subject to all mani-
festations of beauty, even when unexpected.

On April 12, 1904, Léon Bloy and his family
moved out of Lagny and came to live in Montmartre.

The ungrateful beggar had spent four years on the banks of the Marne, greivous years during which he had seen himself abandoned, and a prey to immense fatigues.

Having published the story of his disappointments in Lagny, he published *Mon Journal*, which is that of his sufferings in Denmark.

Mon Journal, the only book by Bloy that, since *The Revealer of the Globe*, did not have a dedication, was rather hastily handed over to the publisher. The title is flat and Léon Bloy has often regretted it.

I will not speak at all about the events contained in that volume; they are all many years anterior to my relations with the author.

In 1904, *Quatre ans de Captivité à Cochons-sur-Marne* came out.

A bookseller in Lagny, M. Bellé, had a very amusing *Coming Soon* advertisement printed up, and covered the walls of the region with it.

On it it said: "Cochons-sur-Marne, it's Lagny," that was inexact.

Cochons was meant to designate Thorigny and Lagny together, and in Léon Bloy's journal, Thorigny becomes *Those from above*, and Lagny *Those from below*.

In that volume of his journal, as in its two predecessors, are contained many sadnesses, but also many funny moments. For those who consider Léon Bloy to be an amusing author, *Quatre ans de Captivité à Cochons-sur-Marne* has got to be Léon Bloy's best book.

The recitation of the author's tribulations is interrupted by extracts of articles and unpublished brochures.

Also found in it is a poem in prose entitled, "Eugène Grasset's Twelve Daughters."

Some people have since supposed that Grasset had been requested by Léon Bloy, who was his friend, to illustrate the poem. It was, on the contrary, Léon Bloy, inspired by Grasset's calendar, who decided to write *Twelve Daughters*.

Eugène Grasset and Léon Bloy knew each other since the *Chat Noir* days. While not having frequented each other regularly, they had preserved amicable feelings for one another.

The first of the *Twelve Daughters* begins with these words: "Is that my grave you're digging?... If it is, hurry it up..."

If Eugène Grasset had had to dig his friend's grave, he would have had to hurry it up in fact, for Grasset died twenty-four hours after Léon Bloy. The last lines of *Quatre ans de Captivité à Cochons-sur-Marne* speak of the author's joy when he finally and definitively departs from Lagny:

"... Change of residence, escape, deliverance..."

He moved to 13, rue Girardon, in Montmartre where he lived for several months only, to relocate again very near to the basilica, rue de La Barre, in a small pavilion tucked away under the trees and a neighbor to similar habitations whose renters were peaceful chaplains.

Léon Bloy, while not very happy in Montmartre, didn't have to encounter the type of hostility that he had endured in Lagny.

In that old corner of Paris, the humblest purveyors have an old habit of putting up with artists and their ways. They are indulgent.

Léon Bloy, who had only enemies in Lagny, was bound to find several men on the butte who could understand him and admire his work.

The sculptor Frédéric Brou and the poor André Dupont were the most faithful of his friends in Montmartre, who were neighbors of the ungrateful beggar, and Brou made a bust of him which will be forever one of the best portraits of Léon Bloy.

A reproduction of that portrait serves as the frontispiece to *Quatre ans de Captivité à Cochons-sur-Marne,* next to a sort of prologue wherein Léon Bloy asks swine, and all those *who walk on four feet*, to forgive him for having compared them *to a category of stinking animals...*

The portrait and the prologue complete that

strange book, resulting from the unexpected contact of the most vulgar provincial villagers with the least common of French writers.

Léon Bloy in Montmartre

After having quit Lagny, Léon Bloy and his family came to live on 13, rue Girardon. Nameless difficulties, not worth mentioning, chased them from there, and in the month February of the following year, 1905, they were installed on rue de la Barre, in too small a pavilion, but otherwise comfortable.

That pavilion was literally buried under the verdure; a sand-covered walk made a tour around it and in order to arrive there, one had to follow a green path that extended from rue de la Barre on the one side and descended towards uncultivated plots on the other. Several habitations, very similar, dotted the length of the path; each one of them had its wooden barrier surmounted by a simple bell.

Nothing more picturesque than that corner of Montmartre where the trees have recently been uprooted and which will be disfigured soon by horrible, modern constructions. When one exited, on certain winter evenings, from one of those rustic houses, the primitive street lamps suspended in the middle of the trees, shaken by the wind, created the illusion of an unexplored hill, at over one hundred leagues from the city.

Rue de la Barre's appearance did not diminish that impression. One had to find its path through a maze of provisory closures made of wood, at times opening up onto what seemed like black deserts containing stacks of planks and piles of stones, at other

times becoming a narrow passageway in which two
people could not walk abreast. The rosary merchants'
shops were hermetically sealed at this hour. Visitors
and, after them, beggars, had quit the neighborhood
of the basilica which was completely surrounded now
by darkness and silence interrupted only by the sound
of the bells. Then one reached the area at the top of
the funicular, where the loud sounds of Paris and its
lights recalled one to reality!

Léon Bloy, when I visited him in Montmartre,
often accompanied me to the esplanade that separates
the foot of the basilica from the entrance to the funicular. He would stop for an instant, look at Paris and
say, "What a lot of suffering in all that! Listen to the
cries! How many of them are cries of grief!"

As soon as he was installed on the butte, he
had continued working in the midst of infinite tribulations, just like in the past, but with real consolations
that were procured by a number of friends. These latter, in fact, had suffered a great deal by the distance
that had been between them, when he was living in
Lagny, and they had been waiting for so long a time
for his return to Paris. To old acquaintances would be
added now new admirations. Léon Bloy's reputation
never stopped growing after that period in time.

I refer the reader to *l'Invendable*, the fourth
volume of Bloy's journal; in it one will see the successive apparitions of Georges Rouault, Georges
Desvallières, Jacques and Raïssa Maritain, Auguste
Marguiller, Ricardo Viñes, Pierre Termier, Léon Bonhomme, and Father Dacien.

I have already mentioned Fréderic Brou who was side by side with Léon Bloy, on a nearly daily basis.

Bloy, moreover, noticed the kind of amelioration that his last books and his return to Paris had occasioned if not materially, at least insofar as his notoriety as an artist was concerned. Personalities in the world of Letters, such as Henry Houssaye or Gustave Schlumberger, addressed their works to him. He wrote to me, in 1906, the following: "For a year now, little by little, I would say that everything is improving... I receive precious testimony in rather large numbers and there is room to believe in a near-term republication of *The Desperate Man*. Then, I will perhaps have the opportunity to heal the wounds that my misery has caused to some..."

The most extraordinary of all those correspondents was assuredly Joseph Florian, the Czech, who had undertaken to introduce Léon Bloy to his country, by translating him.

"What has become of him at this time, the poor Josef?" is a question that Léon Bloy often posed himself in the month of August, 1914.[25]

Prior to that time, from 1901 to 1910, Josef Florian wrote to us, to Bloy and me, touching and picturesque letters, in a French that Bloy qualified as adorable and which denoted an extremely developed artistic sense.

---

[25]Original footnote: I know now that Josef Florian is still alive, in Starà Rise. – R.M.

One might say that that Czech possessed knowledge of the narrative to the highest degree, with a style of richest color, all the while ignorant of the less complicated elements of grammar.

I want to give here some examples of the letters by Florian with respect to images:

> ... *O René, you must be in possession of a copy of* The Revealer *of the* Globe. *I cannot wait to read it and you can satisfy that hunger. Now, I am begging you with all my heart: Loan me that book for a little while! I want to copy it and I want to tell you that you will receive it back again in the same condition that you sent it. And you would be surprised in how short an amount of time you will receive it again. Listen to me, and believe me when I say that I must have that book in my hands and that the situation is serious...*

Having found a second-hand copy of *The Revealer*, I hurried up to offer it to Josef who responded to me immediately:

> ... *I confess that I had no doubt that you would loan me this book, but what you have done, I was not expecting it! What enormous joy! Listen! Do you understand what I am telling you? I will pray to God for you! I have noth-*

ing else to give you in return. For my poverty is quite unique. I left my profession as a school teacher for the state and after several very vain attempts I remain like a stake on the plain. So, I was compelled to weep when I received your gift, which I cannot recompense..."

And later:

... I live in a very small village in a pine forest. No post office! Two lakes, large pastures!...

Given the poverty that he lived with, I could never understand clearly what he did and how he succeeded in translating so many books which could not have brought him much money and all of which are magnificently published.

He wrote to me again as follows:

My friends who, like the stars, from one moment to the next appear and disappear and fall under the horizon, procure books for me... Knowing where to find a million ducats, I would grab them with Heaven's aid. Léon Bloy knows that I am poor, but he knows nothing about my infinite misery and I beseech you to say nothing about it to him in his dangerous state... So, I avow these things to you under seven seals of your silence..."

On one occasion, he had remained for a long time without writing and resumed the correspondence thusly:

Do not be upset!...

His letters, in their splendid calligraphy, were written on fine paper and enclosed in surprising envelopes of various colors and covered by him with bizarre designs drawn by hand. I praised the drawings and asked him if he wasn't an illuminator of books. He responded to me with this brief phrase: "Not an illuminator, perhaps a rubricator."

He affected a strange and naïve brevity as soon as the topic turned away from literature and art. It was in that same way that he addressed to Léon Bloy the strangest telegram that he had ever received. A rich woman from Moravia had become enthusiastic for *La Chevalière de la Mort*, and Josef Florian had hoped that she could come to Léon Bloy's aid. Bloy, finding himself at an extremely difficult and painful moment in his life, had written in substance to Josef: "Tell me whether the person in question gives a favorable response or not. In the contrary case, we will have to starve. Wire me..."

On the following day, Léon Bloy received a wire thus conceived: "Starve... J.F."

In the month of June, 1903, the good Josef had already translated the following: *Ici on assassine... Words of a Demolitions Contractor... Un brelan d'excommuniés... Salvation Through the Jews... The Ungrateful Beggar... The Son of Louis XVI... The*

Desperate Man... La Chevalière de la Mort... The Woman Who Was Poor... not counting Roselly de Lorgues' *Christopher Columbus*. Josef wrote to me as follows:

> *This work continues day after day. But all these translations are still in manuscript form because I do not hope to find an publisher to my taste – the majority are hideous shopkeepers – I loan the manuscripts to men of goodwill who want to read them...*

The only person I know whose enthusiasm could compare to that of Josef Florian is Brother Dacien.

That good brother of the Christian Schools, who came late to Bloy's entourage, had read the books of the master for a long time before knowing him and as his means did not permit him to buy them all, he borrowed them and copied them entirely by hand.

The books that he copied hardly ever left him; he always carried two or three of them on his person, which swelled the pockets of his soutane, and if, when speaking about his preferred author, he had need of a citation, he could be seen pulling out a voluminous notebook, putting on his round reading glasses, and in his harsh voice, reading Léon Bloy out loud.

His method hasn't changed since he possesses the books that he no longer has to copy; he always carries them with him, but I miss seeing him with a duodecimo in hand, that touching gesture of before, and the poor school notebooks covered in blue ink in his regular handwriting.

One cannot say just how much Bloy appreciated friendships and admirers of this sort.

He dedicated *Belluaires and Porchers*, which appeared in 1905, to Florian.

That book was asleep in Léon Bloy's drawers for many long years. It is composed of twenty-four articles that appeared in divers reviews and journals from the time when the author was exclusively a journalist and lambasting pamphleteer. Léon Bloy added a magnificent introduction to it and the text of two small books that had been published previously: *Un brelan d'excommuniés* and *Ici on assassine les grands hommes*.

The delay that was brought to the publication of *Belluaires and Porchers* was due to the successive refusals by multiple publishers who feared displeasing the victims of the lambastor, the which attacked the solid reputations of the Brothers Goncourt, Alphonse Daudet, Paul Bourget, etc...

In 1905, the volume originally proposed to the publisher Stock was accepted immediately and that was a good indicator of the transformation that was occurring then with respect to Bloy's reputation. Almost immediately after the appearance of *Belluaires...* the "Mercure", for the same reasons, asked Léon Bloy for a book of *Selected Pages* which appeared the following year.

The selection of those pages was made by Léon Bloy himself, who included all his works with the exception of *Words of a Demolitions Contractor* because of a kind of apprehension he had, in my opinion unjustified, given that that collection of articles makes for a marvelous book. Each time I spoke to him about it, he told me, "There are a ton of stupidities in those old pages where I demolished myself...!" And when I protested by counseling him to republish *Words*, he was completely surprised: "Really, are you serious?"

To finish up with *Chosen Pages*, I might add that the book is augmented by a beautiful dedication to Mme. Bloy, with a preface by Louis Gatumeau and a portrait of Léon Bloy by Léon Bonhomme; that portrait, which was much talked about when it was on display at the Autumn Salon, is not very natural-looking perhaps, but it does portray in a rather striking manner one aspect of the physiognomy of the "Ungrateful Beggar."

In that same year, 1906, Bloy had published in the *Nouvelle Revue* two important articles on "The Byzantine Epic" and "Gustave Schlumberger." Familiar for a long time with the history of the late Roman Empire, Léon Bloy had absorbed the learned compilations of Lebeau and had often desired that a more Romantic historian could take hold of that subject with vibrant colors and put into relief the impressive facts as well as the adventure of the two Bardas and the reign of Bulgaroctone.

Without approving of Gustave Schlumberger's conclusions, he was enthusiastic for the style that that remarkable writer put to the service of his patient research and saw immediately what he could add, he, Léon Bloy, in a simple general survey furnished by citations. His study in two parts is thrilling.

Never has the superiority of Léon Bloy's religious interpretations been more apparent than in those several pages.

The two articles reunited in one small volume with an illustrated cover was published by Blaizot and, very recently, that little book, augmented by a preface, has been reprinted by Crès.[26]

On August 31, – I return to the year 1906, – one reads the following in Léon Bloy's journal:

"Letter from Termier; he will expect us, on the 7th, at the Grenoble train station, and will give us hospitality in his house in the country, before our pilgrimage. Josef F... will meet us on the Mountain, on the Day of the Assumption."

So, Josef, having learnt of the upcoming pilgrimage by the Bloy family to La Salette, departed from as far away as Moravia, accompanied by a friend, a priest from his country, to meet the man whom he admired on the holy Mountain.

Once again, I send the reader back to *l'Invendable*. Léon Bloy told me later about the en-

---

[26]Original footnote: The title changed. The edition by Crès is entitled *Constantinople and Byzantium*. Vide the two articles by M.E. Bartélemy with respect to that book in the *Mercure*, December 1908 and March 1918.

counter which was bizarre. For Josef had decided to contemplate his great friend without speaking a word.

"It's all the same to me," Bloy told me, "I like quiet people, but to make such a trip to see me exclusively and to spend several days together without our having been able to exchange a single idea, that is what is incomprehensible to say the least, if not aggravating."

Having returned to Paris, Léon Bloy immediately decided to begin the book on La Salette which he had been planning for so long a time and which he was bound to entitle *She Who Weeps*. His intention was not at all to write a definitive historical book, but a work of exegesis in the manner of *Salvation Through the Jews*.

He had to interrupt his work at the beginning, in order to move, the pavilion that he was inhabiting having been condemned for demolition.

Before his departure, he received a visit by M. Dornac who took, there, three very good photographs of him. One of them served as the frontispiece to the second edition of *Je m'accuse*. The three were part of the famous collection "Our Contemporaries at Home," a denomination which made Léon Bloy smile. He let me chose one of those photographs and furnished it with this dedication: "I am not a contemporary and I have never been at home..."

Léon Bloy rented, at rue Cortot, an apartment whose main room was a painter's atelier. I have never seen him so poorly lodged as in that sad and impracticable house. The apartment was on the first floor. It was reached by a narrow stairway. On the landing, there were two doors. One was the door to the lodging, and the other was to the water closet, and as that last door was at least as apparent as the first, it happened that certain, unknowing visitors made a regrettable choice.

The atelier, which was immense, was preceded by two or three dark rooms and one small kitchen. When it was neither too hot nor too cold, staying in the vast room was not disagreeable, but if the summer sun shot its rays through the windows, then it became insufferably hot in that room and one had no other recourse than to descend into a portion of the garden which had no trees in it and which offered only a relative coolness because of it.

During the winter, the atelier was difficult to heat. The rain and even the snow sometimes passed between the interstices of the frame and fell inside, onto the floor. Bloy, refuged between his writing desk and the stove, expressed his disgust for the proprietors.

I confess to having passed happy moments in that miserable hideout. Léon Bloy's good nature, when one could experience it in private, was exquisite. When he spoke with a *proven* friend, as he liked to put it, he let down his armor, let himself go in the joy of showing his entire soul, satisfied his passion of loving and his thirst for blending his religions impressions in with every aspect of his life. He bared his heart of a contemplative and the indifferent man that

he was before giving way to an entirely nuanced being who knew how to discriminate and perceive the
smallest subtleties. He enjoyed the purity of his family, the simplicity of very gentle mores, which he
knew how to surround himself by. His mood was not
variable. Never did I ask myself when going to visit
him, "How will I find him today?" And from the beginning of that period of time, in 1907, I saw him
very often.

I was living in Versailles and each week I
made a trip to Montmartre. On disembarking from the
train, at the Alma station, I took the short omnibus
Place Saint-Pierre-Porte Rapp and, after a slow and
attractive climb, I arrived at the funicular, and then
rue Cortot.

Whether Léon Bloy was waiting to make me
privy to his difficulties or whether he had to announce
a happy piece of news to me, he always received me
with affectionate simplicity. In either case, it was rare
if the day did not end in gaiety.

Léon Bloy's gaiety is visible in many of his
books and particularly in certain parts of his journal,
but it is always as if veiled. Suffering and contemplation, being at the core of his being, made him grave.
He wrote in order to expand souls and to awaken
them, not to amuse himself. If he was rather frequently amusing, it is because he gave himself completely,
and it would have been impossible for him to dissim-
ulate, in his work, that aspect of his character. But it
was necessary to frequent him assiduously in order to
know what spontaneity that good humor had. His

laughter was not provoked exclusively by the comicalness of something he had thought up. I remember a reading we did together of the masterpiece by Marcel Schwob, *Loyson Bridet*.

Léon Bloy burst out laughing, interrupted me in order to laugh some more, no longer hearing a word I said, his arms raised. The book's irony pleased him immensely.

On another occasion, he instigated a reading of Mark Twain and he reserved for himself reading to us from *The Interview* by trying, without succeeding, to stay serious. As for his jokes, they were often made by the contrast of the most extreme individualism and the most ordinary of events.

One day he was pacing up and down in the vast atelier on rue Cortot, coughing in an uncommon fashion, as if he was wishing to make the walls fall down; Mme. Bloy said to him, "Couldn't you cough differently. It's frightening and nobody coughs like that."

Bloy responded, "You would want me to cough like others?"

For some time there was, on rue Cortot, a domestic named Elise who, whether in front of the furnace or leaning on a broomstick, affected an imperturbable phlegm.

I can still hear Bloy, at the moment we were preparing to exit, holding this short conversation with her: "Dear Mademoiselle, in my absence, will you

please be sure more than ever to see to your duty...
And do you know what your duty is?... It is to prevent
criminals from entering!!!" The word *criminals* was
roared and all the same Mlle. Elise remained impas-
sive. Then, Bloy tried again, but this time in a very
gentle tone of voice:

> *It is you, dear Elise, o thrice happy*
> *day,/May Heaven be blessed when it*
> *bends you to my will...*

Then, realizing finally the pointlessness of his efforts,
he turned to me, saying, "She couldn't give a d***!"
and walked with me to the exit.

It is in one of those moments of jesting, at the
cafe de la place d'Anvers, that he said to me one day:

> *In the event that you should write my*
> *biography, I will give you the means*
> *for giving my dear colleagues enor-*
> *mous joy. You will say that I plagia-*
> *rized seven lines... yes, my friend, the*
> *first seven lines of the tale entitled*
> *'Humiliation d'un sublime,' in* Sueur
> de Sang, *– they are not mine.*[27]
>
> *I took them, albeit in a different order,*
> *from the surprising book by Denis*

---

[27]Original footnote: Here are the seven lines in question: "Mais
regarde donc ton jeu, bougre d'âne, t'as la révolution dedans
quinte mangeuse portant son point, dans l'herbe à la vache;
quinze et cinq, vingt; trois borgnes, vingt-trois; trois bœufs, vingt-
six; tierce major dans les vitriers, vignt-neuf; trois colombes,
quatre-vingt-douze; and jouie an un de la républicque, quatre-
vingt-treize. Mon pauvre Auguste t'es passé au gabarit...."

Poulot.[28]

You know that the role of the ass in the fable has never displeased me: "I sheared the breadth of this meadow with my tongue, I had no right to do it..."

So you will tell that to the populations who admire me. You may even add, for you would be talking about Sueur de Sang, *that my first tale in the series,* L'Abyssinien, *is an imitation (you heard me right, an imitation) of Barbey d'Aurevilly...*

I profited from his confidences to ask him, "Are you saying that in *L'Abyssinien,* that that story is not even an anecdote. Did you really know the pale and red warrior, with the face of a girl?"[29]

"Yes," he said to me, "I knew him. He greatly surprised us, and we never discovered where he had come from, who he was, or what had become of him after the war. The portrait that I gave is rigorously exact. Only, he was a foot soldier like myself. I imagined the horse."

We were sometimes interrupted in our conver-

---

[28]Original footnote: Denis Poulot: *Le sublime* – 1872 – Paris, Librairie internationale.

[29]Original footnote: "My so-called Abyssinian had more or less the face of a very beautiful girl, immensely voluptuous and as devoid of courage as can be under the sun..." (*Sueur de sang*). p. 24 in the 2nd ed., Crès, 1914.

sations or our readings by the arrival of visitors, regular or not. The sculptor Frédéric Brou was the one whom I saw most frequently. He had an atelier on rue Tourlaque and hardly a day passed by that he didn't climb Montmartre to visit Bloy or that Bloy didn't descend to see him. They had known each other for many years. Rictus had presented Brou to Léon Bloy.

The latter had been very spontaneously charmed by the artist, whose physique and character were of the sort to impress Bloy.

Frédéric Brou has facial traits similar to those of Baudelaire; he is tall in stature. Previously a non-commissioned officer in the navy, he had kept in his demeanor something of a souvenir of his first profession. He spoke with a deep voice, without severity, smiled willingly, laughed often if life was less bitter. He lived, with his wife and daughter, in his atelier on rue Tourlaque where he had constructed for himself a loft and stairs that went up to the loft. For Brou was as much an architect as a sculptor.

He is also a painter, a mechanic, a secondhand goods dealer, a teacher, a musical instrument maker, a physician, an astronomer, a novelist, and a bit of a sorcerer.

His atelier was furnished tastefully, adorned with exquisite objects, old swords, old images, rare glassware and tableaux of all sorts. Above the piano there was a colored representation of Henri Cros, magnificent specimen of that singular and charming Art.

Léon Bloy often came to take a seat in that atelier; he led me there one winter evening. A large, shaded lamp, suspended at several meters above the floor, shed its light on the plasters and the marble.

"Eh, well!" said Léon Bloy, "how's the sculpture going?"

"Always very badly," responded Brou, "I am also planning to pick up a more lucrative profession soon!"

"Oh! my friend," responded Bloy, "write literature then! You have never wanted to listen to me. You know however that that has been my life for twenty years now!"

After a bust of Léon Bloy, which was very successful, Brou undertook a monument to Villiers d'Isle-Adam which was much talked about during the time it was exposed at the Salon of French Artists in 1907.

A committee was formed and I wont't bore you with the setbacks. Two things are worth mentioning: the small book published by Léon Bloy and the one meeting of the committee in Brou's atelier.

The latter had insisted to members of the committee, whom he knew personally, not to miss that urgent meeting for reasons that it would take too long now to explain. There were about twenty people, among whom Léon Dierx, Camille Mauclair, G. de Malherbe, E. de Rougemont, etc.

Brou, whose role was very delicate, came away from it marvelously. Bloy was terrible. I have never seen him more insolent and contemptuous as he was on that day.

He arrived among the last, bid hello to the several friends that he had; then Brou, placing Léon Dierx before him, said very sweetly, "Perhaps you know each other already?... Léon Bloy, Léon Dierx..."

The author of *Lèvres closes* smiled and very openly held out his right hand: "Hello, Léon Bloy," he said.

Then Bloy, lowering his white and unsociable head, as if he wished to be alone at any price, did not seize the hand held out to him, and uttered clearly "Hello, sir!" before turning his back on him.

One hour later, we were sitting together in a cafe on rue Lepic and I recalled to him the attitude that he had taken: "Yes," he responded, "Dierx is a good man, I am sure of it, and I believe, although his work leaves me cold, that he is also a poet of talent. But why do you want me to know Dierx? Each day he offers that same hand that he held out to me... to Mendès!... to X***, or to Z***. That's his business, but that same hand is not for Léon Bloy..."

As for the small book that Bloy published to encourage subscriptions for the monument and which appeared in 1907, with Blaizot as the publisher, with, on the frontispiece, a reproduction of the model, it is perfect and was found as such by all Villiers' friends and those of his work.

That small book, elegant and now rare, will have been the last testimony of Léon Bloy's persistent admiration for *Tribulat Bonhomet* and *The Future Eve*.

However, *She Who Weeps*, a book that was begun on Léon Bloy's return from his pilgrimage to La Salette, interrupted by his changing residences and by the small book on Villiers, was completed in the following year of 1907.

It was thirty years earlier that Léon Bloy had been initiated into the revelations of La Salette by an old priest who rests today in the small cemetery on the Holy Mountain, facing the basilica.

Since 1878, Bloy had spoken many times of the Apparition, but he had never had the occasion to condemn the attempts made to discredit the Secret of Melanie. His book is almost entirely consecrated to the story of the Secret.

I refer the reader to *She Who Weeps*, in order to deepen his knowledge of that story's origins and its consequences. I should mention here the importance that it held in the life and in the works of Léon Bloy.

For him, all events, in particular and in general, turned on the knowledge or the ignorance of those facts, and he was inspired by it to the last.

In his *Meditations of a Solitary in 1916*, which was his last publication in his lifetime, he returns several times to the predictions made by the Virgin of La Salette, alluding to the passage in the Secret that contains these words: "... then there will be a general war that will be terrible..."

While studying the numerous documents that were put at his disposal in order to write *She Who Weeps*, he had a kind of revelation as to what Mélanie, the shepherdess of La Salette, had been like.

He knew, for a long time, that she was a pious soul and that she had been persecuted by an arrogant and disobedient clergy, but he didn't know that she was a saint and that, in her supernatural life, the miracle of La Salette was merely one episode. Léon Bloy learned of these things with as much joy as curiosity and planned a *Life of Mélanie*, which appeared several years later.

While waiting, having brought *She Who Weeps* to completion, he needed to find a publisher. He sought in the Catholic world of publishers, and it goes without saying that he found none, none among those to whom he had confided his manuscript, not caring to propagate the historical revelations of that denigrator of French bishops.

It was then that M. Termier, to whom the book was to be dedicated, said to Léon Bloy: "Find a printer and I'll pay the costs of publication." Léon Bloy wrote back to him almost immediately:

> ... *The Queen of Heaven was pleased to choose you, you, Termier, to be the stimulator and comforter of her very*

> *minor prophet. To that you add with*
> *all your heart the whelk of angels. One*
> *cannot but congratulate you lovingly...*

Then he procured himself a printer and the work, brought subsequently to the *Mercure*, which accepted it, appeared in June 1908. His success was limited, like that of all his other books, but the goal that he had set out for himself was nonetheless attained.

In religious circles, the story of the miracle of La Salette made rapid progress. Those who had imagined the famous secret buried for good under a column of silence were obliged to declare themselves openly for or against it.

Some understood the importance of that, and Mélanie was no longer merely the little seer of La Salette, but a saint invested with something of a supernatural order, a divine mission. Those revelations, I must say, cannot speak but to a very small number of readers; how many times hadn't I heard Léon Bloy express to me, with respect to his book, his sadness for the modern world which, he said, "is interested only in trinkets!"

"As for myself," he continued, "I will never be consoled to be unable to speak about Paradise Lost with that man that you see over there, with his coffee, two tables away from us. Amongst all these passersby with whom we rub elbows at the moment, how many of them have thought of anything else than their meal? It is intolerable for me to think that there hadn't been one perhaps for whom the name of Jesus was not an occasion for disdain."

When he spoke of the beauty of life considered supernaturally, he did not dogmatize in any way, he was humble.

"We have," he said again, "some magnificent flames to guide us in the *tenebrae*, but what *tenebrae*!"

It was to Mme. Bloy one day that he made that response which so well demonstrated his never-quenched thirst for mysterious things.

"I wonder what your impression will be," she asked, "when you see death approaching."

"Immense curiosity!" he responded.

Considering Bloy in this light, he becomes a unique case.

I know that men, in rather large numbers and throughout time, have disdained the present life and placed all their desires in the unshakeable hope of a future beatitude; but I do not believe that a single one of those believers had pushed that sentiment as far as Léon Bloy had and above all under such strange conditions. If those men in effect were able to sustain stubborn battles, feel themselves cruelly threatened, outraged, persecuted, they did not create for themselves, like a pleasure, a framework for their suffering that was in constant contradiction with that very suffering.

Léon Bloy was an artist, a being made to

charm other men; he had all the resources of a creator of joy and beauty, and he did not wish to use those gifts except in the achievement of a work consecrated to the glory of God. Consequently, he passed before his contemporaries like a stranger. People misunderstood his attachment to sorrow, which was a voluntary attachment whence came the rarest and best of what he wrote.

Those who did not understand him saw in him merely a man impossible to satisfy, an *ungrateful beggar*, as they said, without realizing that they had given him the title to one of his most beautiful books.

But let's not forget to add that that dolorous man was capable of incomparable joys: "The tears of sadness," he told me, "turn quickly into tears of love!" And if he loved deeply, he was deeply loved. With what care, what constancy, did he want to profit from the affection that was lavished on him. One might say that he reserved the treasures of sensibility for the moments when his tenderness could manifest itself and when he could apply himself to make those instants as frequent as possible.

He repeated a hundred times a day, almost on every encounter with his daughters: "There she is, there's my dear little Véronique," or "Hello, my dear little Madeleine!"

An absence lasting half an hour in Montmartre gave him the occasion, on his return, to go and embrace his children, and he never failed to do so.

And I have often said to myself, on seeing him

live in this way, as he pleased, that he must have suffered a great deal when he was living on his own in
dreadful Paris.

How heavy they must have weighed on him,
the smiles and the handshakes of men of letters, however great or small, on that strange colleague who had
to give his entire soul or remain irremediably closed.

The continuous correspondence contained in
his journal can only confirm that observation. He either opens up entirely or he puts out a blunt refusal,
sometimes insolent and oftentimes comical.

His unpublished correspondence will soon be
published; one would have to reproduce his calligraphy in its entirety so as to show at what point he refused to give himself to the first person who came
along.

His writing did not reveal it until after an exchange of several letters.

He was anxious, besides, of any novelty for
fear of what it might contain of the banal. And for
that reason, he preferred the sorry aspect of his poor
neighborhood, in Montmartre, to new and comfortable streets. And when, fed up with his atelier on rue
Cortot, Bloy decided to find another apartment, it was
with the intention of staying close to the basilica, to
the place du Tertre, and above all to the Church of
Saint-Pierre whose solid architecture seemed so well
suited for harboring his prayer of an old primitive.

Léon Bloy didn't have to move out of his atelier on rue Cortot until the month of October, 1908.

While waiting, his visitors became more and more frequent; he was even obliged to reduce them by spacing out some and suppressing others: "I have become a curious animal," he said, "I do not want that."

Sunday was for the most part his day of reception. I went there very rarely on Sundays, much preferring to find him alone with his family. He was really himself on those instances of confidence, his sadness always tempered by that internal peace which is particular to deep souls, which never abandons them and the constant interest that he had for his friends. Questions that were too general in nature, and the latest news, both left him indifferent.

It was on rue Cortot that I saw, for the first time, Ricardo Viñes and André Dupont. The first, already in possession of his reputation, had only a few moments of free time. He came, when he could, to lunch with Léon Bloy who loved him a great deal. All the artists who frequented Ricardo Viñes know the irresistible attraction of his impulsive, generous, indulgent character, of his erudition and of his spontaneous outbursts of almost infantile joy which betrayed too happily an inalterable simplicity and cordiality.

When he began to play at the piano, at Léon Bloy's house, he stayed there as long as he needed to play through his admirable repertoire.

Bloy who was no more a musician than Flaubert or Gautier, listened to Viñes with sustained attention.

At first, he sat not far from the piano, crossed his legs and joined his hands together on his knee, with a resigned attitude. By the second morsel, one could see his face brightening, as if he were himself surprised by his musical sensibility; then, all of a sudden, his vision became very clear, his eyes were fixed on the keyboard and Viñes' fingers. By the second chord, he stood up saying, "This Catalan is a marvelous artist."

Ricardo Viñes came regularly to present his warm wishes to the Bloy family on the first of each new year. He came with his arms full of gifts. The games destined for Véronique and for Madeleine were tested out by Viñes himself, in the presence of everyone, and his boisterous laugh interrupted his demonstrations every minute.

Completely different was the character of André Dupont who also frequented rue Cortot at that time and who, having become Bloy's neighbor not long afterwards, remained one of his most regular guests until the latter moved out of Montmartre.

Dupont had a guttural voice in perfect analogy with the type of rictus that a solidly fixed monocle made run across his clean-shaven face. With that muted, but mordent voice, he uttered rough aphorisms that were found to be excellent criticisms. Bloy, ever the demolitions contractor, fully enjoyed those short phrases, punctuated by brief exclamations that denoted more insouciance than nastiness.

André Dupont had a lot of wit and a great deal of talent. The little silhouettes that he published a little bit everywhere, and particularly in *l'Intransigeant*, made one regret that he had not written more; his admiration for Bloy was enormous.

Bloy had him write a preface to the fourth volume of his journal, but above all he loved his conversation which was filled with anecdotes and tittle-tattle on a large number of people whom Bloy did not know, in contrast to his friend who knew all the literary milieux of Paris and was brilliant in the descriptions that he made of them. We often descended the three of us, Bloy, Dupont, and myself, from the heights of rue Cortot down to the exterior boulevards.

Léon Bloy was no longer content then with a simple escort to the funicular. He accompanied us down the stairs and, having arrived at Saint-Pierre square, we took the small rue Steinkerque to the boulevard and we entered a cafe that faced place Anvers. In that cafe, I encountered Georges Rouault many times, often accompanied by Léon Bonhomme, whom I spoke about earlier with respect to the portrait that adorned Léon Bloy's *Pages choisies.*

Bonhomme proposed a game of billiards to Bloy who almost always accepted.

Rouault, one of the best human beings and one of the most intelligent artists I have ever met, gave the impression of being a refractory, said "bonjour" with a nervous twitch of his head, while looking into the distance. He remained silent for a long while, then all of a sudden took part in the conversation and proclaimed things of great commonsense with the same gestures and the same emphasis as if he were speaking with some extravagance. He sustained paradoxes as well, but with the simplicity of tone ordinarily given to the most wise of theses.

The quasi hebdomadary reunions at the cafe on the place Anvers were not usually so numerous. Many times, it was just us three, Bloy, Dupont, and myself. And at those times, the conversation was principally literary.

When Bloy stirred up old memories, the name of Barbey d'Aurevilly returned frequently to his lips; he recalled his old friend's generosity: "How's that! Bloy, your shoes have holes in them and you didn't tell me! That's not good!"

When he repeated this story, Bloy wept.

I cited to him passages from *The Bewitched* or the *Chevalier des Touches* and I saw, by the emotion that he felt, how much he must have admired Barbey, how strong his first enthusiasms must have been.

"At that time," he said to me, "if I had to write about d'Aurevilly, I always felt myself beneath the task and I would have admired anything about him..."

He spoke to me also of Paul Féval and made me read *Annette Laïs*: "It's a charming thing," Bloy said, "beside so many mediocrities. Féval wrote too quickly, he hurried through his books. The man was excellent. He walked kilometers through Paris, even though he had bad legs, to bring me some assistance. 'Here you go, young man,' he would say, 'take that and don't let my wife know.'"

Bloy admired Féval as a novelist or Gozlan because their procedures were as different as can be from his own. He was never an arranger and he never wanted to write a novel. He called *La Femme pauvre: a contemporary episode*, in order to mark the difference between that strange book and a novel.

"One must bring things to a close," he said. "*The Human Comedy*, that prodigious and exact vision of an author who does not want to finish, who limits his effort to being nothing more than a vision, utterly disillusions me."

However, he knew that a noble or profound idea can appear from a simple arrangement. Thus the manner of old novelists, while giving him the impression of a worn-out and misleading thing, procured for him pleasant surprises that he wasn't ignorant of.

It is for that reason that he found recreation from time to time by reading a novel by Walter Scott, Féval, Erkmann-Chatrian, or Gozlan.[30] He asked me one day to loan him *Balzac intime*: "I would like to reread," he said to me laughing, "the story of the horse eaten by the rats..."

When he returned the book to me, he con-

---

[30]Original footnote: One has often refused to accept Bloy as a critic. The exceptional worth of the novelists that he read and that he enjoyed begins however to come to light. One will soon see the injustice done to him.

fessed, laughing again, that it had really amused him. "I had need of that!" he added.

I spoke to him of Stendhal, asking him if he had reread *Le Rouge et le Noir* and *La Chartreuse de Parme.*

He responded: "No, but I would read them again willingly; I don't particularly like the spirit of those books, but they are strong books. And *La Chartreuse...*, it's still a memory from childhood for me."

For there was also in those desires to read, a manner of rediscovering impressions of his former intellectual life.

Léon Bloy noted that in *Le Vieux de la Montagne* with respect to Walter Scott, "... all of whose novels," he wrote, "end by excellent marriages and to sentimental readers' satisfaction, with one exception, I think, that of *Lucie de Lamermoor.*"[31] Bloy was more than happy to mention that last work. He recounted, by way of example, a very fine dramatic situation wherein Edgar cries out: "... I am armed and I am desperate... Everyone leave!"

"And Léon Bloy added, while holding up his fist, 'everyone leave, you heard me right... everyone... leave!'"

On October 3, 1908, I received the following note:

Dear friend,

---

[31]Original footnote: p. 161 of *The Old Man on the Mountain*.

Several words only. We are in the middle of making arrangements to move out, which ought to happen Tuesday.

Our new, very nice abode is, will be, from now on, 40, rue de la Barre, where you visited in 1906, but not the same pavilion. You will be surprised.

Yours,

– LÉON BLOY

It was a question, that time, of a large ground-floor apartment rather bizarrely done, along which wound a paved courtyard which ended at a very small garden surrounded by walls whose roughcast, having fallen off years before, had large black and green marks on it. The paved courtyard, with its tufts of grass and its rivulet running alongside the dilapidated building was as charming as one could imagine. Mme. Bloy raised ducks there, whose distraught quacks welcomed visitors. When Bloy returned home, he said bonjour to the aquatic birds and smiled at his baroque lodging.

It was truly the *Ungrateful Beggar*'s abode, which pleased him and which he regretted leaving.

His study was at the back of the courtyard with a French window from which Léon Bloy could watch the main entrance.

Another window gave onto the small garden. The room had a high ceiling and had a severe appearance. The walls, a bit somber, were relieved by some prints and by the yellow desk surmounted by shelves in the same color. Desk and shelves had been brought from Denmark to France by Léon Bloy and had belonged to his father-in-law Christian Molbech.

There is still today, in Mme. Bloy's possession, a photograph representing Christian Molbech's study. One can recognize Bloy's desk in it, and the singular armchair whose seat is long like a pirogue and hard like a camp bed.

Into the wood of the desk where he leaned, next to his blotter, Léon Bloy had carved the following phrase with a penknife: DILIGENTIBUS DEUM OMNIA COOPERANTUR IN BONUM.[32]

In the middle of the table, facing the writer, there was a Christ surmounted by a large crown of thorns and, next to the Christ, a statuette of *She Who Weeps* purchased at the time of his first pilgrimage. Since the *Ungrateful Beggar* until the last lines of his journal, all Léon Bloy's books have been written at that desk and also the large number of letters of which many, alas! were requests for assistance. Those last were subscriptions loaded with indications, tall and thick: URGENT, VERY URGENT, VERY PRESSING!...

On the shelves, the books were arranged in perfect order; books of history above all remained within reach: Schlumberger, Henry Houssaye, Norvins, Vandal, etc.

In a small, special bookcase whose glass was

---

[32]*Diligentibus... bonum*: See entry January 25, 1914, in *On the Threshold of the Apocalypse*, where this phrase is mentioned.

protected by curtains, Léon Bloy hid several rare editions from profane eyes.

A little bit everywhere, in the house, one saw the prints by Eugène Grasset and a large number of photographs of paintings, of which one was the *Sacré-Cœur* by Georges Desvallières with a dedication by the author, a violent work that Bloy was greatly taken with.

Bloy at times affected to grow disinterested in what was adorning the walls of his house: "I want to give all this away," he said, "I begin with you, what would you like, choose?"

"But no," I said, "you won't give any of that to me, or anyone else; it is absolutely necessary that you keep it!"

"What does that mean?" he replied.

"That means," I said again, "that you are an artist and that you need some drawings and color around you."

He responded by shrugging his shoulders: "Perhaps you're right... it's quite pitiful!"

I saw sometimes, wandering about under and between the furniture, an ill-tempered little dog with a fantastical looking shape to its body that Frédéric Brou had wanted to copy as a model for a gargoyle. Every now and then Bloy threw it a morsel of sugar... under the bed and was amused by the animal's contortions as it squeezed its lumps between the wooden frame of the bed and the parquet.

Like the atelier on rue Cortot, the dimensions of the room obliged Bloy to spend enormous sums of money on coal, and frequently. Eight months out of the year, his stove was red; he took responsibility himself for maintaining the fire. "The cold," he said, "is my greatest enemy!"

He fought his greatest enemy with an incessant surveillance, interrupted his reading to run to the coal box, returned holding the poker in one hand, and in the other hand was a shovelful of coal that was gobbled up. And Léon Bloy went back to his study while rubbing his hands with a satisfied air.

Delivered, in his own words, from the vermin of rue Cortot, he published *l'Invendable* and *Blood of the Poor*.

The first is the continuation of the author's journal, journal which includes everything, from simple notes addressed to suppliers or pettifogging proprietors, to the noblest and most touching prayers. It has been correctly remarked that in *L'Invendable*, Bloy speaks frequently of his readings and that Napoleon and his historians interest him more and more.

L'Invendable, published by the *Mercure de France*, enjoyed the relative success of prior volumes of his journal.

The proofs were hardly corrected when Léon Bloy began that book on *Money* which he had so often entertained his friends with.

No other work by the author was carried out with more vertiginous rapidity; in two months, it was fully written, corrected, and published, I do not know why, by the publisher Juven.

In the Preface to the *Old Man on the Mountain*, which appeared in the *Mercure de France* in the following year (1910), André Dupont spoke for a long time about *Blood of the Poor*.

I cite the following lines from the preface by André Dupont:

"In order to write a new book, Bloy merely had to listen to that rumbling sound in his ears, those fierce and thin years that dogged him for so long a time, when he wandered alone in search of his soul.

"*Blood of the Poor* is written in an absolute will of hatred and execration for the rich: '... Everyman who enriches himself sells the Christ. One cannot become rich except by selling the Body and the Blood of Our Lord Jesus Christ.' Such is the tone of the book."

Bloy sent me a copy with this dedication: "These pages were used to wipe the knife!"

The contrast between those violent expressions and the author's life, at the moment when he wrote his book, elicited surprise in those who did not know his past and could not account for that infernal existence that he had led and the provision of observations that he had made.

At the time when he published *Blood of the Poor*, he still had ennuis and cares, but as I have already mentioned, the quality of his life had improved, he could work with tranquility and he profited thereby, for he loved working.

Holidays interrupted it, and it must be said that from 1908, the moment that *L'Invendable* came out, to 1913, they increased. Léon Bloy visited successively Créteil, Le Tréport, Sainte-Mesme, Cayeux, le Nouveau-Brigton, Binic, Taille-Petit and Saint-Piat. And the more holidays he went on, the more he detested holidays.

To go on holiday in that way into the unknown was odious to him. He went more willingly when he was visiting a friend, when he knew that the arrival and departure would be softened, that he would not have to ask for his trunk from an employee whose hostility overwhelmed him with sadness and disgust. One had to have seen Léon Bloy in a train station, his baggage claim ticket in hand and saying in an imploring as much as an unheard voice: "Monsieur employee, will you get my bag for me?" in order to understand how a vulgar event of that sort could throw what he called so precisely his infantile mind into disarray.

He sat back down at his writing desk. With what art he knew how to express, not only his suffering, but the ridiculousness of what he had to suffer. As he knew how to reduce everything that his con-

tempt made him disdain to the most minuscule proportions.

That did not stop him from remaining on all
occasions true and respectful and making an effort to
understand what instinctively was not suitable to him.

His relationship with music and musicians
were, from that point of view, surprising and conclusive.

Léon Bloy did not like music. I am not speaking about religious music which he enjoyed with the
simplicity of his Christian heart, nor the small impro-
visations by his daughter Véronique which, by their
brightness in innovation and expression, were really
those of Léon Bloy.

I mean to say profane music, that of
Beethoven and Debussy.

I have shown Bloy's attitude listening to his
friend Viñes. Even still, that had to do with very inti-
mate gatherings, at Léon Bloy's home, at Jacques
Maritain's, or mine.

On another occasion, I saw him, not without
anxiety, attend an entire concert of the *Messiah*, by
Handel, given in Trocadéro.

The performance was organized by Raughel
and Borrel, two friends of Bloy, which the latter
would have been afraid of saddening by not accepting
the invitation that they had made to him. And I was
afraid that that long and slightly theatrical concert

would be fastidious to him.

His impression was huge and favorable to the point that he wanted to attend a second performance, fifteen days later. I saw him at the exit and we were able to speak for an hour afterwards: "My friend," he said, "I followed all that with an emotion that never stopped augmenting while that marvelous poem unfolded before me. I wept at certain passages. I applauded those excellent artists. I made no more effort to understand Handel than I did formerly when listening to the unattractive voice of my poor Villiers, when he accompanied himself on the piano."

Madeleine Bloy's entrance into the *Schola cantorum*, studying violin, the relations that followed with the master Vincent d'Indy, kept those good dispositions alive in Léon Bloy.

We could hear the progress that his studious daughter was making over time. Beside Ricardo Viñes, we also heard the violinist Eugène Borrel. Finally, Mme. Brou reminded Léon Bloy of the time of his debuts, singing in a charming voice something by Rollinat:

L'âme des fougères s'envole...

Bloy did not hide his joy for those musical gatherings, in his house at Montmartre, gatherings that ended ordinarily by him reading something.

Seated at his desk, Bloy took one of those small, grey-covered notebooks where, in a fine and condensed calligraphy, he kept his work in chronological order.

He held the notebook in both hands and brought it very close to his face. He read in a calm but firm manner, with an intonation that was very appropriate to the things that he had written. His pronunciation was clear, but particular. He spoke as best he could in an old French style, saying *escayer* for *escalier*, *coyer* for *colliers*, *Moyère* for *Molière*, etc.

Those readings took place also in Versailles where he came two or three times a year, to my place or that of his godson, Jacques Maritain.

I would go to wait for him at the Rive-Gauche train station. He arrived with his walking stick in hand, dressed in a slate-gray suit and wearing a soft felt hat; he put on his *pince nez*, looking for me from a distance.

After we arrived at my place, he joked. He ironized, expressing commonplaces... on purpose, and laughed after saying them: "It's a beautiful spring day!" or "I have so many things to tell you!"

I responded in the same vein, "Did you have a nice trip?" He laughed again. Then, all of a sudden, he said, "Before we go to your place, let's first go get an aperitif."

We headed to a cafe located on rue Royale, across from the Orangerie, a mediocre but very popular cafe.[33] Bloy took his seat, asked for a bitter and

[33]Original footnote: Bloy would have gotten a good laugh out of it, if he knew that his cafe had become the seat of a Credit

pulled out of his pocket a small cigarette lighter which he used when the cigarette that he was smoking was on the verge of going out.

In those face-to-face conversations, he had no bitterness about him and let his true nature come out. He spoke about his disappointments even but with a good humor, and he was the first to affirm the improvement of his lot. He said, "Ah! I can see some years ahead without any suffering; I've paid my dues for such a long time now!" He repeated it several times: "Ah! yes, I've paid my dues!"

At my place, lunch was prepared according to his taste, easy enough to do. He loved being served a leg of lamb sliced at the table. "It's a very French meal," he said. He was also served his favorite dish: potatoes fried in oil with garlic.

He chewed the morsels of fried garlic like the true Meridional that he was.

During the meal, he often leaned towards the window, searching with his eyes his friends the trees, in the neighboring garden.

Two or three times, I brought him to the park, despite his repugnance for everything Bourbonian and for Versailles in particular. I made a point of not showing him the palace and the collections, but I knew that the Trianons would charm him, as ruins are known to charm melancholic imaginations. I led him then towards certain solitary corners of the park: "Ad-

---

company.

mit it," I said to him, "not everything in Versailles is dreadful, am I right?" He responded: "This place is lovely, very nice,... are you satisfied?"

Léon Bloy however would prefer not to go outside, but to listen to music instead, or to read us pages from his books.

I asked him one day to choose, from among the stories he had written, one that he had worked the most on, from the point of view of form. Without hesitating, he chose a story from his *Histoires désobligeantes*: "Cain's Most Beautiful Discovery;" and then, from *Sueur de Sang:* "At the Conquerors' Table."

In the evening, as he left Versailles he went to the train station accompanied by all his friends, for it was not rare for him to ask Jacques Maritain to meet him at my place, or that Frédéric Brou should accompany him.

On the following day, or the day after that, he wrote me to tell me how much he had enjoyed himself.

In the month of December, 1909, I found myself over for lunch at the Bloys, in Montmartre. With me were Viñes and the abbot Petit, a priest of great intelligence and rare erudition. All three of us, we waited for the afternoon reading. Bloy had a notebook on his desk opened to the first page.

Before beginning, he gave this small discourse more or less:

"You are waiting for something by Léon Bloy, but it is not Léon Bloy whom I am going to read to you... You do know, don't you, how much I love Termier. That great scholar is one of my most loyal friends, I have dedicated *She Who Weeps* to him.

"Perhaps you do not know that Termier is a poet and that he cannot write, even when discussing a scientific subject, without betraying the sensibility of a very fine and very touching artist..

"But what you absolutely do not know is that his daughter, Jeanne Termier, is herself a true poet, and that she has just communicated to me her admirable verse, which I want to write a preface to, for they are going to be published soon.

"I have to say that I had a most agreeable surprise when I read her verse. I knew, of course, that it could be interesting, but I found myself in the presence of a work of genius.

"Finally, Jeanne Termier had warned me of the presence, in her book, of a certain number of *vers libres,* and I have often manifested my disdain for *vers libres*.

"Today, I confirm that this entire little volume, *vers libres* and all the rest of it, is absolutely remarkable... What's more, you're going to see it for yourselves!"

And Léon Bloy read to us, in its entirety, *Derniers refuges,* and we were enthralled.

He went to a great deal of effort to nuance that verse with so personal and profound a charm.

Several days later, he communicated to me the very curious preface that he wrote for *Derniers refuges*, and the critics who have analyzed those poems have completely ratified the praises that Léon Bloy lavished on Jeanne Termier.

I say that that preface is curious because Léon Bloy judges poetry as a layman; he does not discuss the literary merit of the work even once. A short time later, he expressed to his friend Alfred Pouthier, the author of *Soliloquies*, his ignorance of poetic language.

"When it happened that I needed," he said, "to write on Baudelaire, Verlaine, or Jeanne Termier, you must have admired the unusual virtuosity of my reticences and how much I excel at expressing absolutely nothing at all. It's quite simple really, I do not *know*!

"When someone presents a poem to me, my first reaction is to run in the direction of my wells, the wells of my soul, if you like!..."

On the subject of which, I said to him, "Have you never written verse?"

"Yes," he responded, "I have written detestable things in that genre. Corbière would have said that my verse was lined up like lead soldiers. It did not sing at all!"

And he told me the unusual story of a poem

that he was asked to write for a review.

The poem was entitled, "The Solitude of God." Bloy wrote thirty or so lines of verse that he destroyed almost immediately afterwards. He confessed to me that he had preserved nothing of that attempt which had made him renounce versification forever.

The end of the year, 1910, was marked at Léon Bloy's house by the arrival of Peter Van der Meer, a Dutch man of letters who had converted, with all his family, to Catholicism because of Bloy's books.

Bloy was ravished by those abjurations which were added to so many others that he had also instigated.

Four years earlier, it had been that of Jacques Maritain, his young wife, and their sister Vera Oumansof. Of all Léon Bloy's friends, Maritain was one of the master's most cherished. A constant and dogged labor kept him away, more than either of them would have wanted, from our amicable gatherings where I did not often encounter him.

Jacques Maritain, more than ever attached to his philosophy and his teaching job, is, for all that, recompensed by his work. Very young and already looking very old, admired and loved by his students, armed with a holy doctrine that he expounds with marvelous clarity, he is among those rare individuals whom his adversaries themselves are obliged to render justice to.

And Léon Bloy, that old artist, enemy of philosophy, came many times to listen to the conferences given by his dear godson, which he came away from both stupefied and moved.

As for Van der Meer, I saw him, one evening in November, in Bloy's study, when he came for the second time.

He was a tall fellow, a bit silent, who however had no difficulty expressing himself in French; but he contented himself at that time to look at Bloy with the avid eyes of an innocent who would dream of being devoured.

Van der Meer recounted the story of his conversion in a very passionate book, which appeared in 1917, published by Crès, with an introduction by Léon Bloy. That book is not just a recitation of the author's conversion, it is filled with memories, and the memories of his younger years are those of a refined, almost voluptuous artist, whom the scenes of nature and life never leave indifferent.

It makes one regret that other books by Van der Meer have not been translated into French, novels that earned him a writer's reputation in Holland.

Léon Bloy published, in his journal, a very beautiful letter wherein he recounts all the details of Van der Meer's conversion.

These friends, he wrote, *never stop*

saying that their conversion is my work or at least that I irresistibly influenced it.

It is as if Our Lord was kissing me on the lips, with his adorable Mouth. It is as if his mother, my Lady of Compassion, had taken me into her arms and was holding me close to her heart... I don't know how to express it...

That is what I wanted to say to you. And now, I don't know what else to do than to embrace you tenderly, entreating you to embrace your dear children for me.

– LEON BLOY.

From then on, the Van der Meer shared, together with Jacques Maritain and his family, the role of Léon Bloy's godchildren, which role they conserved until the last moments of their beloved godfather's life and which they continue to conserve even today, with respect to their godmother.

Léon Bloy, before moving out of Montmartre (he took his leave on January 16, 1911), published the next volume of his journal and entitled it *The Old Man on the Mountain*.

I remember trying to dissuade him, with all my powers of persuasion, from using that title which I found had been used previously a large number of times; but Bloy was thinking of his dear mount of La

Salette and didn't want to listen.

As for the book itself, I believe it is worthy of its predecessors, and I want to add this: it contains the "letter to Letellier."

I have never met that Letellier, of whom I am completely ignorant, but given it is to him that we owe that exquisite thing, we will keep the memory of Letellier for Eternity.

You can read that marvel on page 360 of *The Old Man on the Mountain*.

Bloy was unhappy to leave Montmartre. I saw him several times before his departure. We made the trajectory once again from rue de la Barre to place d'Anvers. Dupont, as far as I remember, was with us. It was about five o'clock in the evening. Kids were playing up and down the stairs running parallel to the funicular.

Two of those children had set up a kind of teeter-totter on the iron handrail.

When Bloy, who was in a bad mood, passed by them, the extremity of the board came and struck the edge of his hat. He turned around sharply, almost angrily, brandishing his walking stick: "What have we here," he said, "what sort of way is that to behave; I will strike you with my stick!" I can still see the frightened faces of the two boys, who looked like something right out of an album by Poulbot, the one boy sitting on his plank at the foot of the steps, the other dangling in the air and Bloy before them, magnificent and terrible, his cane raised!

Recently, I was curious to return to rue de la Barre, to see what had become of that quarter since Bloy's departure.

I crossed, not without some emotion, place du Tertre and I entered into the smoke-filled room of a cafe where Bloy often led me; I retook the route that we often took, rue Lepic, rue Cortot. Arrived at rue de la Barre, I found only demolitions and ruins.

I have had to reconstruct from my memories the small iron door, the shrill-sounding bell, the paved courtyard, the ducks' quarters, the window of the eating room, the modest table mounted on its trestles, and I have seen my old friend again, for a fraction of an instant, saying the *Benediction*, which he followed by another prayer that he had learnt among the Carthusians. He articulated clearly in a deep voice, very beautifully: "... *Edent pauperes et saturi...*"

# # #

My dear friend, René,

I have something that will please you. I received from Périgueux the little portrait of my charming person, executed by myself at 19 years old.

I have to tell you that I was surprised – others will be too – by the incredible finesse of that drawing which I have not seen for over 40 years and which shows me what I looked like in 1865.

That image would certainly amaze Elisabeth. That's all I have to say.

You will have an extraordinary thing in it, but the photograph must be perfectly executed and before your very eyes. *I do not want that memory, the most precious memory that I have from my beginnings, to be entrusted, for one single hour, into improper hands.*

I do not dare mail it to you even. You must come then and see it, which will be easy for you to do in this spring season.

I embrace you and your world,

– LÉON BLOY

Léon Bloy in Bourg-La-Reine

"I will have moved!" Léon Bloy said to me, after he had been forced to move out of rue de la Barre. "And, for all that," he took up the subject again, "I would still like to see that corner of a cemetery where I will repose!"

The "Ungrateful Beggar" prophesied this time, without realizing it. It was in Bourg-la-Reine that he was bound to die.

I have already said how much he liked Montmartre. A month after his departure from the Butte, he wrote about it again bitterly to his friend in Tours:

> ... *I have often moved, but there was never a more painful uprooting. We had grown quite fond of living in the shadow of the Sacré-Cœur, immersed, several times a day, in the sonorous waves of its great bell. We lived in a quiet house, all to ourselves, far from the sounds of the street, exclusive possessors of a lovely garden where I lovingly cultivated some flowers, where my wife raised some fowl. All that is over. No more geese, no more ducks, no more poultry, no more dog, but above all, oh! above all, no more basilica! We find ourselves now in a*

bourgeois apartment, however large
and comfortable, but so banal! The
church, very close by and sufficiently
welcoming, does not displease us, but
there are no longer the so very numer-
ous masses of our dear Basilica. We
are separated from those friends of
ours whom we could see every day
and the incessant sounds of the neigh-
borhood here torment us. We are a lit-
tle sad then..."

My hebdomadary visits were however easier than before. Léon Bloy proved to me his desire not to see
them become rare by organizing my itinerary: "It's
quite nice," he told me. "Once arrived at the Montpar-
nasse train station, take the metro, then the tramway,
and you can be here, in Bourg-la-Reine, in about 2
hours."

"You will depart at 6:10 pm. A nearly direct
train will bring you back to Versailles at 7 o'clock.
There is a small cafe very close by the train station, I
will see you to your wagon..." And it happened as he
said, until July 1914 when the means of communica-
tion became difficult for the reasons one knows.

These last years in the life of Léon Bloy
showed no change in his ways, unless he had become
more attached to his work than before.

The polemicist that he had been no longer existed. He paid no attention to the praises that were
lavished on him, which became if not very numerous

at least more frequent.

Léon Bloy who, long ago, collected all the published insults lodged against him, and few writers will have been steeped in them as much as he was, became completely disinterested in compliments and admirations.

He kept at home many scrapbooks containing invectives lodged against him: "I was very fond of that filth," he said sometimes. As for encomiums, he disdained them and had but very few occasions to respond to them or to discuss them consequently.

Léon Bloy often received small books that some of his friends thought might interest him. He kept two or three at most, from among the more or less ridiculous ones, which he wrote notes in the margins of, and those rather special criticisms appeared in his journal.

Everything else was tossed into the wastepaper basket, and Bloy often accompanied the gesture with this phrase, which recurs sometimes in his writings: "Life is too short!"

Once however, the title of a booklet caught his eye. It was this: *The Perils of the Faith and Discipline in the Church of France at the Present Hour*, and the author was Mgr. Turinaz, bishop of Nancy and Toul.

The work had one hundred pages. Léon Bloy began reading it attentively and picked up his quill with the intention of making notes on it.

The ideas that he encountered were not bound to displease him. Mgr. Turinaz wrote, in sum, against modernity and mediocre laics who were involved in introducing modernism into the most widely-disseminated Catholic newspapers. Bloy had often expressed his contempt for both.

Unfortunately, Mgr. Turinaz was not much of a writer, had made the mistake of being unfamiliar with Léon Bloy, and went to great efforts to distance the most energetic and violent images from his expressions.

"I have obeyed," he wrote, "no feelings of malevolence with respect to people..." His work was, alas! the very opposite of lambast.

From the third page, he let escape this imprudent phrase: "I speak, because no other voice has made itself heard." Léon Bloy, with his blue pencil, wrote in the margin what seemed to say: "Eh well! And me?" The first half of the small volume contains principally exclamation points and underlinings.

From page 39 on, Bloy's patience is frayed by the prelate's gentleness: his notes betray his impatience.

By page 40, Bloy wrote, "When I read the word *mentality*, I lose all courage; I am completely done for."

Then Bloy has continually the air of saying to Mgr. Turinaz, "I am absolutely in agreement with you, but you do not know how to shout that, you understand diddly squat about bawling out!"

It is fitting to remark here that none of those annotations were addressed to the bishop's text, but to the authors he had cited.

On page 82, Bloy explains himself, "This gentleman here," he wrote, "has the good fortune of falling into the so very uncruel hands of Mgr. Turinaz. In another person's hands, he could have been dealt with in a somewhat more serious fashion." Several days later, Bloy gave me the booklet to which he had added the following envoi:

> *Pardon me, my dear Martineau, to have soiled with my annotations, some of them indecent, this small book which I confess to have read disrespectfully. But you are so passionate for me that I supposed, injuriously perhaps, that that would not displease you.*
>
> – LÉON BLOY

Then he said to me, "I know that you are a bit of a bibliophile, take it!"

Afterwards, I had the small volume bound in bishop's violet and placed it on the shelf next to Léon Bloy's works. It does not constitute the least curious of his fantasies; but it is not as indecent or as disrespectful as Bloy says, when one considers that none of his notes were destined for publication.

Some people have spoken with insistence on Bloy's invectives with respect to the Catholic clergy. On this point, a common understanding and definition of the word invective would be in order.

Bloy has sometimes shown a certain ridiculousness or lapse, together with a vengeful complacency, but he never went so far as to utter invectives at priests.

I have always seen him behave respectfully in conversations that he had with them – even when they were not his friends – and he received them amiably. To a vicar of his parish who said to him, "You are always a lion. Couldn't you sometimes act like a sheep?" he said "But no, for then, I would eat myself!"

Bloy practiced invective on his colleagues. *Belluaires et Porchers* and *Je m'accuse* contain very violent instances of it; but his *journal*, and it is above all from his journal that one has drawn the wherewithal to reproach him, – his journal is never harsh except when the author reproduces an incident exactly as it occurred, or words exactly as they were pronounced, but can those be called invectives?

And then, is it so paradoxical to sustain, as M. Arbelet has done with respect to Stendhal, that hateful expressions, from a person who is gifted with an excess of sensibility, are indicative of an overabundance of feeling.

While one accused Léon Bloy of being born to hate, of having cultivated his hatred, he said, "I was born for feeling; nobody has loved men as naïvely as I have..."

And what would give even more weight to M. Arbelet's observation is Bloy's admiration for *Le Rouge et le noir* which he qualified as a vigorous book and which he preferred to *La Chartreuse de Parme*.

The 18th century spirit, met with in Stendhal, was hateful to him for literary and philosophical reasons; but the excess of individualism was not displeasing to him.

He even expressed, rather well, that need for hatred because of feeling when he said to me, "... They go and cut the throat of the lamb or the ass of the fable... I hurl myself at the exterminators in order to cut their throats... Dear me! and then they accuse me of lacking in charity..."

* * *

His setting up house in Bourg-la-Reine happened rather rapidly. Léon Bloy expressed, once again, his desire for tranquility. All his friends received a printed card thus conceived:

> *Change of Address*
>
> *M. and Mme. Léon Bloy have the honor of informing you that from May 15, 1911, they will be domiciled at 3, place Condorcet, Bourg-la-Reine.*

*Please do not encourage useless visi-
tors.*

When I asked him, "But what do you mean by 'useless visitors'?" he responded, "Those visitors who
have neither a mind or money. They must bring one
or the other... or both!"

Jesting was never beneath him and, as he grew
older, he jested more willingly than formerly.

People have accused him scatology. It's the
least false and least stupid of accusations brought
against him, not because he essentially was a scato-
logue or that he had limited his manner of jesting to
that single genre, but because it is certain that he
rarely let escape the opportunity to express himself in
that manner, even when he ought instead to have con-
strained himself.

There is, on place Condorcet, in Bourg-la-
Reine, a mediocre bust of Condorcet that a disrespectful municipality had placed in front of a public urinal.
When Bloy saw that, he said to me: "In several years,
they will construct another public urinal on the other
side of the square... and it will be my bust that they
place before it."

Although he was indifferent and disdainful, he
was also too much the artist not to be observant. In reality, nothing escaped his eye, in the places he frequented. The regulars at the cafe Lecoq, in the square
before the train station, had no idea of the interest
Bloy paid sometimes to their activities. In winter, we
spent one hour at that cafe, waiting for the departure

of my train. Bloy brought a book along and said to me: "This here is for when you depart... This cafe is very good, but it does not have a checkerboard!..." He called out to the owner M. Coq: "... Don't you want to buy a checkerboard, Monsieur Coq?"

During the summer, one sits in the garden where there were two beautiful trees and chairs painted blue, a garish blue, which made Léon Bloy, every time he saw them, say, "But what a singular (he pronounced it *singuyère*) idea to paint the chairs like that. It's awful!"

To get to this cafe, walking from the train station, one must pass before the statue of André Theuriet who was, for a certain period of time, the mayor of Bourg-la-Reine.

The author of *Raymonde* is represented seated, in a languorous pose, holding a rose in his hand.

When Bloy gave a rendezvous to a friend, with instructions to come and find him at the cafe Lecoq, he never failed to give the following directions: "You will pass before a mediocre statue of a ridiculous man, then you will see the trees and the blue chairs and finally you will see me, me, with my friend Martineau, and perhaps also my godson Pierre..."

From time to time, at cafe Lecoq, I found those who used to join us at place d'Anvers: André Dupont, Léon Bonhomme, Alfred Pouthier.

Ricardo Viñes sometimes came to cafe Lecoq.

He came by train, from Massy-Palaiseau, and re-counted his lunch with the painter Odilon Redon.

When he wanted to tells us his impressions, Bloy, guessing in advance, cried: "Bad, he is very bad!..."

I will not speak about the numerous holidays Léon Bloy made: he has related all that in his journal. As for myself, I paid him only one visit, outside of his ordinary habitation.

I went to see him in Saint-Piat, in 1912.

Saint-Piat is a small town several leagues from Chartres, with a stop on the Paris-Brest line. The village is uninteresting. Bloy stayed where the route to Chartres begins, rather pretty at that location be-cause of the river and the trees that border it.

Despite the somewhat uncomfortable lodg-ings, Saint-Piat did not displease Bloy. It was from the time of Bloy's first visit to that hole of a country village that Bloy's correspondence began with Au-rélien Coulanges, then director of *Marches de Provence*, a small review that showed promise, but that was interrupted by the war.

After several letters, a plan was elaborated such that, thanks to Coulanges' activity, a special is-sue would be consecrated to Léon Bloy. (See an as-sessment of that publication in *The Pilgrim of the Absolute*.)

One will find in the same volume of his journal the story, too short in my opinion, of another holiday he spent, in Périgord. Léon Bloy told me of his emotion on seeing again Fenétreau, that faubourg of Périgueux, where he was born and where he returned so often when his parents were still alive, that same Fenétreau where he led Georges Landry, whose old willow trees he had drawn formerly, on the banks of the Isle river and which he found completely changed: "The night of modern embellishments has descended over all those luminous things," he wrote magnificently.

All the time that he spent on those holidays, Léon Bloy worked, and he only hoped for a prompt return to Bourg-la-Reine in order to continue working. He was extremely encouraged by the republication of several of his books. *The Desperate Man* had an edition republished by *Mercure* and another one by Crès (The Masters of the Novel Collection).

The same publisher republished *Sueur de Sang*, l*es Histoires désobligeantes* and, during the war, *The Byzantine Epic*, which appeared under a different title: *Constantinople and Byzantium*. Finally, the publishing house *Lettres Françaises* reprinted *Je m'accuse*.

Léon Bloy was very sensitive to the successive requests made to him by the publishers. "If," he told me, "I can no longer benefit by the commencement of justice, at least I think that my children can one day!" And that half-success further augmented the internal peace and welcoming gentleness that became the most apparent traits of his character, as they had been the very foundation of his nature all along.

Although he always was, as he said, armed to the teeth, he had changed a great deal since the day I had, for the first time, met him in Lagny, fifteen years earlier. That change occurred very gradually. Bloy himself ended up by having a notion of it. Mme. Bloy was the principal author of it.

After having shown her husband the boundless admiration that he was avid for, she organized for him a home and hearth which is indispensable to the artist who has as much need of a safe harbor as other men, having nothing to expect from the outside world but disillusions.

If the suffering of an artist of Léon Bloy's caliber is measured by the greatness of his work, one can say that all his life he had a need to be consoled.

Mme. Bloy's task required much more than tenderness, it necessitated a great intelligence. Léon Bloy's wife had, more than any other woman, that superior intelligence that was needed for the complex role she needed to fill, and she had it to the point of adding sometimes to the work of the Master and to his genius.

Bloy knew it, said it, citing many a time her whom he called his collaboratrice.

For, if throughout the world there were many beggars who, in their lifetime, were never classified as ungrateful, it has often been noticed that their gratefulness was never shown towards those to whom they owed it the most.

Léon Bloy, himself, never forgot anyone, not even those who loved him, and if posterity really knows what role it has to play, it will conserve for Mme. Bloy the place that Léon Bloy had given to her.

The first volume published by Bloy after his arrival in Bourg-la-Reine was that of the *Life of Mélanie, Shepherdess of La Salette, Written by Herself*, the manuscript of which had been communicated to him by a priest.

The reading of those pages had been, for Léon Bloy, who had always proclaimed Mélanie's sanctity, the sweetest of revelations. The book was published in 1912 by the *Mercure de France*.

Mme. Rachilde published, with respect to it, an article full of enthusiasm in *Paris-Journal*. That article, entitled "The School of Silence," gave Léon Bloy enormous joy. He sent to me by mail the issue of *Paris-Journal* and, not long afterwards, he said to me, almost crying: "What really struck me about Rachilde's article is that it is not my introduction or my own style that moved her, but Mélanie's life, the saint's story!"

The publication of that book was almost immediately followed by that of *The Soul of Napoleon*.

What to say about this last work?

Apart from *The Exegesis of Commonplaces*, no other insuccess is comparable to the insuccess of

The Soul of Napoleon. Readers will find that book in-comprehensible, disconcerting, incomplete even.

For those who are used to Léon Bloy's books, all those reproaches are unjust. Léon Bloy did not approach Napoleon any differently than usual.

Léon Bloy never saw anything but the Soul, his soul and the soul of others. In individuals as in deeds, he searches exclusively for what is mysterious. Napoleon could not be understood by him until he had looked at and studied the soul of Napoleon. The title, to mention it in passing, is splendid. For those who do not know Léon Bloy, for those who bought that book merely in order to find what an ordinary historian could have written on a like subject, I understand their stupefaction even more. And yet?...

What is so surprising about a discoverer of enigmas who approached that incomprehensible emperor who had so often charmed poets, in order to try to explain him, without retelling his story, but armed however with a documentation that the best critics of history have not discussed.

Ed. Barthélemy in the *Mercure* and Guy de Cassagnac in *l'Autorité* have published, the former principally, more than a sufficient number of pages to demonstrate to the public the importance of Bloy's work. Nothing doing. Nobody wanted to listen. Some wanted Hugo, others wanted Stendhal; the best they could say to the author of *The Soul of Napoleon* is, "So, you are Bonapartist." Léon Bloy responded, "That is discouraging!"

And after his book on Napoleon, he sought a diversion to his studies of history, by writing a second series of his *The Exegesis of Commonplaces*. Some of his best friends recommended to him that new attempt which he gave himself over to, despite the insuccess of the first.

The author and his friends were satisfied by the result, proclaiming the superiority of that second series over the first. I confess that I don't share their contentment. In my opinion, it is in the first book that one will find the most powerful and richest pages.

When Bloy asked me about it, I told him my thoughts and he immediately replied, "It is because the first book was dedicated to you that you say such things!"

I must add that, while not being a success, which would not prove anything however, the second volume of *Commonplaces* sold better than the first.

That was above all due to Léon Bloy's growing reputation. Not only were his books beginning to be reprinted, but publishers sought him out, tried to obtain from him unpublished material or some forgotten article.

Thus did Bloy entrust to M. Laquerrière, for his collection of literary curiosities, all his articles on Huysmans, which the publisher of *Belluaires et Porchers* had not wanted, finding them too vehement. That resulted in a small book entitled: *On Huysmans' Tomb*.

On Huysmans' Tomb is divided into two parts: "Before the Conversion" and "After the Conversion."

Léon Bloy's friendship with Huysmans was, in the beginning, very close; the booklet that I just cited proves it, at least the first part does. Léon Bloy's articles on *À rebours* and on *En rade* constitute the finest praise that anyone has written on Huysmans' work. The latter writer was, moreover, extremely touched, and, when they appeared, he wrote letters of thanks to Bloy which shows the reciprocal trust that existed between the two artists. Their letters will be published one of these days.

My only regret is that Bloy, later, had tried to diminish his praise, vainly accusing himself of having been mistaken with respect to the two novels of exceptional worth, which he had been the first person to understand as they deserved. Even more, one must regret the defection by Huysmans, who, by not naming Léon Bloy in an essential and influential interview, caused the rupture.

Several weeks after the publication of his booklet, Bloy had begun a new volume of his journal, *The Pilgrim of the Absolute*, when the war broke out.

The Bloy family was at Saint-Piat since July 8. Myself, I was in Versailles during the same epoch. We remained without any news of each other until August 10 when I received the following letter:

Mévoisins, near Saint-Piat.

Dear friend,

I entreat you, write to me if you are still alive. In our profound solitude, from which we cannot exit, for lack of money, we know nothing save the fragments that the journals inform us of. But we see that the events are enormous, unprecedented. It's the probable expiration of the great Term. Perfectly isolated and without any resources, menaced to die of famine, except for a miracle, we would like at least to know something about our friends.

Having received my book (The Pilgrim of the Absolute) *extremely late, I can no longer distribute it but to a very few. Anne-Marie should have received a copy and Madeline another. Did they arrive?*

Impossible to send you your copy printed on Holland paper, which has come too late, impossible to satisfy Elisabeth and many others.

We are rather miserable.

According to what we can understand, Wilhelm seems to have set out poorly. His mustaches are at risk. If my wishes are fulfilled, that sinister cretin will end up in a pile of excrement.

Write me, for the love of God.

– Léon Bloy

I responded immediately and, on September 8, another letter by Bloy informed me that he and his family had quit Saint-Piat in order to go to Rennes where they sojourned for the entire month of September.

Returned to Saint-Piat, they were chased away by the cold on October 17 and returned to Bourg-la-Reine.

We were able to see each other not long after that. I found Bloy at work: "I have begun," he said, "a book on Joan of Arc and Germany; it's my way of fighting; I would prefer the other way. I would love that, in fact, but I no longer have the strength!"

In June 1915, Léon Bloy experienced the first signs of an illness which he was to suffer from for more than two years and which he must have died because of. One morning, he came to lunch with me in Versailles; I met him, at the *Rive Gauche* train station, leaning on Van der Meer's arm and walking with difficulty. He was pale and complained of pain on his right side. Mme. Bloy had accompanied him, with Van der Meer.

We made him sit for a moment, at the cafe; he didn't want anything to eat or drink, lit a cigarette, but smoked it with visible displeasure.

In the afternoon, he felt better little by little and was able to return home at the end of the day. But we were all concerned by his pallor and extreme exhaustion. He had to be taken care of, often kept to his bed, was deprived of his quotidian communion, listened to the counsels of his doctors, followed a regime and all that on top of the disquietudes caused by the war; he aged a great deal. His weakness increased.

His book, *Joan of Arc and Germany*, had appeared the previous May 8. The sales were non-existent or nearly. *Joan of Arc and Germany* has some similarity to *The Soul of Napoleon*. One can sense the same procedure of investigation, after a complete documentation, a procedure that was misunderstood in both books' case.

An admirable article by Edmond Barthélemy, which appeared in the *Mercure* on July 1, succeeded in giving Léon Bloy some comfort. With the article having been cited by Léon Bloy in his Journal, I do not wish to cite it again in its entirety, but I need to extract the following lines:

> *From which results a very moving, and so clear, reading. So clear. Like all Léon Bloy's books, moreover. The events have only confirmed the writer in his manner of feeling and expressing himself. But he was always, in his other books, what we see him to be in this one. He has always had, for want of extraordinary events like those of today, his own reasons, the events of his soul. The intensity of emotion with him has always so irresistibly carried the clarity of expression. Bloy is a seer*

of the moral world. Emotion and form, the one in its profundity, the other in its lucidity, announce the unparalleled energy of his intuition, of what must be called his practical sense of the Invisible, which is the only reality...

In that sphere of the Invisible, I will pause only at what is sentiment, the life of the heart. Ah! it is here, I have to say, that it is so delicious to listen to Bloy express himself with that same clarity. *I have always thought that the author of "The Woman Who Was Poor," in all that he has written, addresses himself above all to our hearts. Women are the best judges of this, and I have seen them, I have seen mothers of families, whom his books have attracted. This writer, who does not flatter women, inspires confidence in them. They are advised of a loyalty that is in him, they feel the rectitude and the authority that is in his thought. They know that there is a gentleness in him, which they can trust.*

M. Edmond Barthélemy is completely right and it is rather curious to remark, after the lines that precede, that anteriorly to M. Barthélemy's articles, it was only women who wrote about Léon Bloy, pages that were truly worthy of him and his work.

Mme. Bloy, Rachilde, and Mme. Termier-Boussac have written, in fact, the only articles that might be compared to those by Edmond Barthélemy, as to Léon Bloy's intelligence and his extraordinary books.

Although ill, Bloy continued to work however and, during the summer of 1915, he prepared the 7th volume of his journal *On the Threshold of the Apocalypse*, which he gave to the *Mercure* at the end of the year.

For the first time, it was not possible for him to bring the work in person to his publisher.

Alfred Vallette came to Bourg-la-Reine to take possession of the manuscript.

The physician counseled Mme. Bloy to look for a house with a garden attached to it. Holidays now were impossible for the poor ill man that Léon Bloy was from now on, and the open air was indispensable to him. At this time, at Bourg-la-Reine, there was in fact the house previously inhabited by Charles Péquy. Mme. Bloy immediately secured it.

The habitation was not very comfortable, or rather there was only a dining room, which was spacious enough to allow for conversations at leisure. Still, Bloy didn't have at hand his writing desk nor, consequently, his journal, his manuscripts, or other marvels which he used to communicate so affectionately and so deftly. But, around that habitation, there was a splendid garden, very vast, where the old trees cast a beautiful shade. During the summer, a table was set up in the shade and dinner was served there.

Bloy was happy, but his health did not get any better.

All throughout the year of 1916, terrible catastrophes happened, one after the other, to the people of his entourage.

In the month of March, André Dupont, soldier in the 4th regiment of zouaves, was killed by the enemy. Then there was Philippe Raoux, captain of artillery, and finally Jean Boussac, who also fell in the field of honor. All three were among Léon Bloy's closest friends. He was devastated when he heard the terrible news each time. In the *Bulletin des écrivains* (the April 1916 issue) he finished the article that M. Divoire had asked him for, on André Dupont, with these words: "... I am ill these last several months, ill of course from all the horrors that come to us these last two years, and this last blow was not what I needed to get better." It is certain that the war hastened his end and that his physical pain was made worse by an immense bitterness and great compassion.

Something similar to the mental shocks found in *The Desperate Man* or the *Ungrateful Beggar* were attacking the old writer, but without shaking his confidence in sacred promises.

Grief wrested from him a last cry of hatred against the enemies of his Fatherland, at the same time as an act of faith, and it is with the hand that death was already making tremble that he wrote one of the most beautiful books that he had written.

Meditations of a Solitary in 1916 can stand up in comparison to *Salvation Through the Jews* and *The Woman Who Was Poor* or *Sueur de Sang*, that is to say with the finest and most striking of all that Léon Bloy has written.

I will never forget the emotion I felt the day he read the first chapter of it to me: I AM ALONE... His feeble voice, his face ravaged by grief, his thin fingers, everything indicated a near end. By a last and noble effort of the will, he had put all his art into some phrases that expressed the solitude of his soul. And to read those phrases at that moment in time, as he did, it was of incomparable grandeur but also of infantile simplicity. One could hear his groaning, but one saw his desire, that curiosity nearly with which he spoke about death.

The form of those *Meditations* was so well suited to Léon Bloy that as soon as his book was published, he began another of identical format but the latter was less vibrant than the first.

The title, *In the Tenebrae*, perfectly indicates the manner in which that work was composed and realized. Bloy's strength was diminishing more and more.

He continued to work, and to recomfort his friends, speaking to them of the mystery, until the day when he completely lacked the strength.

On April 6, 1916, he wrote to Georges Joubert, a new friend:

> *My dear friend,*
>
> *It is a sick man that writes to you...
> with difficulty. The last two months
> have been very hard on me and today
> the delay of spring continues to make
> me suffer a great deal. My greatest
> sorrow these holy days is to be unable
> to attend the great offices [of the
> Church].*
>
> *I dragged myself to church yesterday
> and this morning only to return com-
> pletely exhausted. Such is the news
> that you ask of me. I think a great deal
> on death with the regret of not having
> lived better.*
>
> *May God bless you for the good that
> you do for me. I received your photo-
> graphs with pleasure. Your girlfriend
> is very lovely, and I can only congrat-
> ulate you with all my heart, while ask-
> ing that it please God to give you what
> has been promised through his angels
> to men of goodwill: peace on earth.*
>
> *As for happiness, the which consists
> however – in my opinion – in enduring
> for God the worst of torments, I do not
> dare speak, so terrible is the vision
> that I have before me...*

These last words show us that he was always the prophet. Perhaps a little later one will want to collect everything he announced, all the prophesies scattered here and there throughout his work.

The events we have just gone through make certain predictions of his all the more impressive. One need only consult *The Byzantine Epoch*, which appeared in 1906; on page 21 of the 2nd edition, one finds this:

> *"... In all history, no story is more heartrending than the seizure and sack of Thessallonica by the renegade Léon Tripolitain... In several hours, the famous city was turned into a burning charnel house. The Tripolitain led twenty-two thousand young people of both sexes into the most terrible servitude, a treatment reserved for the masses of our delicious Christians which the Bazaar of Charity has not sufficiently clarified..."*

In the same volume, and consequent to the same date, he wrote again (page 105 of the 2nd edition):

> *... One knows that in 989, the princess Anne was married to the dreadful Vladimir... She went to live among those terrible barbarians (the Russians), the dirtiest men that God has created... They were the same in 1814. They haven't budged since then and*

what a folly to hope that those Scythi-
ans, kept for ten centuries in the most
abject servitude, suddenly freed will
go and govern themselves sagely while
kissing the hands and feet of a consti-
tutional autocrat...

When I left Léon Bloy, in the month of June 1917, he said to me, knowing that I would not return until the month of October: "Perhaps we will see each other again?" He saw death coming for him, with great calmness, and without changing his manner of being, speaking of his book, of his projects, everything just like before, joking freely, listening with emotion to the stories of those of his friends who were soldiers.

In the dining room or in his garden, he sat for long periods in his chair, his hands crossed over his knees which were also crossed.

Between meal time, he tried to eat some bread or drink some wine, as was his habit. He selected croutons from off the table that he threw to a big old silent dog that M. Paul Léautaud had given to him, now that Léon Bloy lived in a house with a large garden.

Bloy had taken an affectionate liking to that big dog and gave him all the names ending in "or" that came to mind: Hector, Agenor, Antenor, Victor or, by abbreviation, *Tor*.

Léon Bloy's visitors were comparatively fewer than before. Pierre Van der Meer was one of the most assiduous during those last months.

The painter-engraver Henri Boutet, whom Bloy had known since *La Plume*, around 1890, lived in Bourg-la-Reine and was a good neighbor to his old buddy.

Another painter, this latter one very young, Charles Bisson, came often, during that time, to the house of Bloy, whom he esteemed, and he felt that he was understood by that enthusiastic and deeply Christian artist.

Finally, Henry de Groux found his way again, he also, to the Bloy household, and the last trip that Bloy had made to Paris was to visit the exposition that his friend had set up on rue La Boëtie.

My absence dragged on through the entire summer, and during that time I received no letter from Bloy. I concluded thereby a worsening of his condition. I was not mistaken. Having returned to Versailles, on October 26, 1917, I received the following message the following day from Mme. Bloy:

> *Dear René,*
>
> *Your friend is very ill. I was always hoping for the best. Seeing his strength rapidly decline, I'm letting you know so that you aren't devastated if God took, any moment now, his old, weary servant...*

I immediately ran to Bourg-la-Reine where I met Alfred Vallette who had been, like me, forewarned.

When we entered into the dining room that Bloy no longer quit, – they had moved his bed there, – it was impossible to hide the gravity of our friend's condition, who felt lost and spoke of his near death with great courage.

The following day, he had received the Last Unction and Communion. He held out his hand to us and began speaking with difficulty; his respiration was weak and his articulation difficult. He was in pain.

And yet, he succeeded in expressing himself, in order to hold a conversation with me, as before, about the book he had been working on, that had been interrupted, chapters of which I did not yet know anything about. Also, as before, he joked. While he was half-extended on a sofa, he remarked that in the past he should have played the part of the... Récamier![34]

Then he returned to his serious and melancholic thoughts. The sun was setting, and when I raised the window curtains to give him a bit more light, he said to me, "It's dark mostly in my heart and in my mind."

On Friday, November 2, I could see him for only an instant. His traits had changed a great deal from two days earlier. "They say that I'm getting better, but I have no more strength." That November 2 was his last day. God wanted to grant to the dead the

---

[34]the... Récamier: in reference to a particular type of sofa or divan, but also, jokingly, to the beautiful socialite Madame Récamier, who gave the sofa its name, and who is painted famously as reclining on the same.

supreme prayer of Léon Bloy who had so often invoked Him for them.

From time to time, Bloy leaned on the arm of a friend and took several steps in the apartment.

He went from a chair to an armchair, from the armchair to the sofa where he extended himself and tried to get some sleep.

It was during one of his short naps that Léon Bloy very gently passed away, amongst family, on Saturday, November 3, 1917, towards six o'clock in the evening.

The obsequies took place the following Tuesday. Despite the matinal hour and the difficulty of communications, the funeral cortège was considerable.

The funeral procession was led by the writer's widow and daughters, and around them were grouped Alfred Vallette and Mme. Rachilde, Charles Grolleau, M. and Mme. Jacques Maritain, M. and Mme. Van der Meer, M. and Mme. René Martineau, Elisabeth Joly, M. and Mme. Brou, Pierre Termier, Mme. Termier-Boussac, Henry de Groux, Elisabeth de Groux, George Auric, Ed. Souberbielle, Ch. Bisson, G. Rouault, Adolphe Van Bever, Georges Landry, E. Barthélemy, Auguste Marguillier, Adolphe Willette, Mme. Bienvenu, etc.

At the church, the ceremony was very simple, very dignified, and it was in radiant sunlight that Léon Bloy's body was conducted to Bourg-la-Reine cemetery.

According to his wishes, there will soon be, on his tombstone, a bas-relief of Our Lady of La Salette.

May these several pages demonstrate, to those who dream of a more complete and definitive biography of Léon Bloy, what that genial artist was like during the last eighteen years of his life when I had the joy of knowing him and spending time with him. One will recognize in him an honest, affectionate, solitary man, of a ponderous mind and full of bravery, whom neither the injustices nor the poverty that he faced had prevented from achieving the most original, eloquent, and powerful work of our era.

His complete works, while entering into literary history, will be Léon Bloy's best defense in the face of posterity.

One will find therein a great disdain for conventions and propriety even, that is certain, but beside the invectives that he has so often been reproached for and which, moreover, will one day be found to have been justified, Léon Bloy has put into his work enough faith, beauty and love to explain the attachment and recognition that several souls have for him and an admiration that can only grow and that soon will be indisputable.

Figure 1. A photograph of Léon Bloy's grave in Bourg-la-Reine, taken May 2022 by the translator. The plaque above the author's name is that of La Salette, with her head in her hands, weeping.

Other Books by the Publisher

Fanchette's Pretty Little Foot by Restif de La Bretonne

Je M'Accuse... by Léon Bloy

My Hospitals & My Prisons by Paul Verlaine

Salvation Through the Jews by Léon Bloy

Words of a Demolitions Contractor by Léon Bloy

Cellulely by Paul Verlaine

Ecclesiastical Laurels by Jacques Rochette de la Morlière

Flowers of Bitumen by Émile Goudeau

Songs for Her & Odes in Her Honor by Paul Verlaine

On Huysmans' Tomb by Léon Bloy

Ten Years a Bohemian by Émile Goudeau

The Soul of Napoleon by Léon Bloy

Blood of the Poor by Léon Bloy

Joan of Arc and Germany by Léon Bloy

Theresa the Philosopher & The Carmelite Extern Nun by Marquis d'Argens & Anne-Gabriel Meusnier de Querlon

A Platonic Love by Paul Alexis

Two Novellas: Francine Cloarec's Funeral and Benjamin Rozes by Léon Hennique

The Revealer of the Globe: Christopher Columbus & His Future Beatification (Part One) by Léon Bloy

Héloïse Pajadou's Calvary by Lucien Descaves

An Immodest Proposal by Dr. Helmut Schleppend

The Pornographer by Restif de La Bretonne

Style (Theory and History) by Ernest Hello

On the Threshold of the Apocalypse: 1913-1915 by Léon Bloy

She Who Weeps (Our Lady of La Salette) by Léon Bloy

The Sylph by Claude Prosper Jolyot de Crébillon (*fils*)

School of Woman by Nicolas Chorier

Voyage in France by a Frenchman by Paul Verlaine

Ourigan, Oregon by William Clark, Richard Robinson, and anonymous

Drowning by Yu Dafu

Cull of April by Francis Vielé-Griffin

The Misfortune of Monsieur Fraque by Paul Alexis

Fêtes Galantes & Songs Without Words by Paul Verlaine

Joys by Francis Vielé-Griffin

The Son of Louis XVI by Léon Bloy

Septentrion by Jean Raspail

The Resurrection of Villiers de l'Isle-Adam by Léon Bloy

Poems Saturnian by Paul Verlaine